CONTENTS

'A' projects a larger image on the retina because it is nearer than 'B'. Due to size constancy both 'A' and 'B' are perceived as the same size, however.

PERCEPTION

How do adults make sense of what they see? A naive view suggests that objects in the external world appear as images on the retina and that is the end of the problem. There are difficulties here; for instance, the size and shape of the retinal image vary according to how far we are standing from them. The nearer an object the larger its retinal image – yet as we move about objects are always perceived as being the same size, despite the constant variations in the dimensions of their retinal images.

The same problem exists for shapes; objects appear to maintain their shape despite the constant change in the shape of their image on the retina. A coin on a table projects different shapes on the retina according to the direction from which it is viewed. Viewed from vertically above the retinal image shape is a circle, viewed at an angle the retinal shape is an ellipse.

How is it that the constantly changing retinal images give rise to the experience of a stable world of objects which maintain their size and shape?

The seventeenth-century continental rationalist philosophers, including Descartes, argued that human beings are born with the ability to see the world in the same way as the adult. The British empiricist philosophers maintained that we literally have to *learn* to perceive the stable world of objects.

Hamlyn all-colour paperbacks

William Barnes-Gutteridge

Psychology

illustrated by Whitecroft Designs

Hamlyn · London

FOREWORD

Psychology is concerned with the study of man; how he thinks, remembers, learns, feels and understands. It also has something to say of man in society; his personality and his departures from normally acceptable behaviour as, for example, in mental illness. It will soon become evident on reading this book that psychology, although it does have a large subject matter, has not progressed very far, and most of the answers it does offer are very tentative. The hope remains, however, that this little book will give some of the reasons why this is so. The study of man is very difficult and it calls upon the resources from many disciplines and many types of mind: from the insights of Freud, through work on animals, to some of the modern developments in computers and neurophysiology.

The writing of a book inevitably involves many people, and I should like to thank in particular Terry Dutton of Whitecroft Designs, who was responsible for most of the illustrations; his patience, good humour and cooperation were greatly appreciated. Thanks are also due to Elsie Cross who typed the manuscript. I should like to dedicate this book to Sue, Mark and Tim.

W. B-G.

The illustration on page 64 is reproduced from *Book of Life* by kind permission of Marshall Cavendish.

Published by the Hamlyn Publishing Group Limited
London · New York · Sydney · Toronto
Astronaut House, Feltham, Middlesex, England

Copyright © The Hamlyn Publishing Group Limited 1974

ISBN 0 600 37020 8
Phototypeset by Filmtype Services Limited, Scarborough, England
Printed in Spain by Mateu Cromo, Madrid

The visual world of the newborn infant

How *does* the newborn infant perceive the world? Does he see a stable world like the adult? Or is it a world which is so confusing and unstable that the infant has to learn to compensate for changes in shape and size of the retinal image? This latter opinion was the view of most psychologists until quite recently.

T. G. R. Bower of the University of Edinburgh, in a series of ingenious experiments, has presented evidence which supports the view that young infants in the first six to eight weeks of life already possess the ability to compensate for changes in the size and shape of retinal images. It seems from Bower's evidence that the shape and size constancy mechanism (which maintain the shape or size of the perceived object despite changes in the retinal images) are probably innate, and the newborn infant perceives the world as Descartes suggested: as a stable world of objects.

Bower's apparatus produces virtual intangible objects which appear solid, when viewed through polarizing goggles.

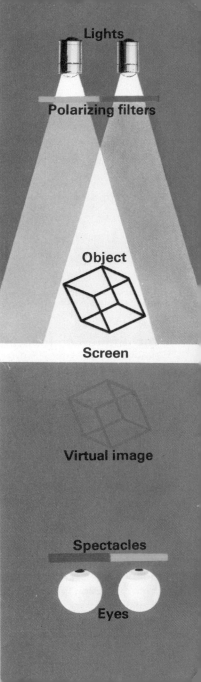

Lights

Polarizing filters

Object

Screen

Virtual image

Spectacles

Eyes

Virtual object

A baby wearing polarizing goggles attempts to grasp a virtual intangible object in front of a screen, during Bower's experiment.

The infant's conception of solidity

How does an infant acquire the concept of solidity? Does the infant have to learn that every time it sees an object it is solid and not intangible, or is it born with this ability? One influential view which stresses that it must be learnt states that the ability to identify the solidity of objects by sight is one of association between the sight of the object and the information gained by touching it.

Bower has recently suggested that the concept of solidity is innate and not learnt by a process of association. He devised a method to produce 'solid' objects which are in fact not solid, but illusions of solid three-dimensional objects produced by polarizing filters.

A plastic translucent object is suspended between the lights and the screen so that it casts a double shadow on the back. If the screen is viewed from the front using polarizing goggles, these double shadows merge to appear as a single 'solid' three-dimensional virtual object in front of the screen. It is a virtual object because attempts to grasp it will result in simply clutching air – it has no real existence.

In his experiment Bower fitted infants, aged between sixteen and twenty-four weeks, with polarizing goggles and placed them in front of the apparatus. Each of the babies was presented with both real and virtual objects to grasp. None of the infants showed any surprise at touching the real solid objects, all of them, however, showed surprise and even distress when presented with the virtual intangible objects they could not grasp. It seemed then, that they expected the object to be solid.

This experiment suggests that if the concept of solidity is not innate, it must be learnt in the first sixteen weeks of life.

The perception of depth

Gibson and Walk have shown that the perception of depth in humans and animals is very probably innate. When babies who are old enough to crawl are placed on a wide bridge of solid transparent glass (a 'visual cliff') through which it is possible to see a drop, they refuse to crawl across and make for the safety of the side. This is also true of the behaviour of most newborn animals, which also refuse to cross.

Gibson and Walk's visual cliff. Children and young animals refuse to cross the glass through which a drop is visible.

Viewing an upside-down world

At one level perception involves the transmission of nerve impulses from retina to brain. The brain must also interpret the information it receives, however. The image on the retina is not a faithful replica of all that we consciously perceive. For instance, we perceive another person as always being the same size and shape, despite the fact that as he moves the image of him on our retina varies.

Another puzzling fact which was noticed by the seventeenth-century British empiricist philosopher Berkeley in his *Essay Towards a New Theory of Vision* is: If the image on the retina is upside-down, how is it that we see it the right way up? In 1896 George Stratton, an American, conducted an experiment to find out what would happen if he continually wore an optical system that produced retinal images the right way up. Stratton wore this system during all his waking hours. At first the world did appear drastically altered, the world appeared inverted and Stratton experienced great difficulty in performing even simple tasks. By the fifth day, however, he was able to walk around his home with some ease, and he reported that it was only by a conscious effort that he was able to remember that objects were upside-down.

When Stratton removed his inverting system on the eighth day he wrote:

'. . . the scene had an air of strange familiarity. The visual arrangement was immediately recognized as the old one of pre-experimental days, yet the reversal of everything I had grown accustomed to during the past weeks gave the scene a surprising bewildering air which lasted for several hours. . . .'

Certainly Stratton's experiences and behaviour had changed over the week: initially the world did appear strange to him, and he experienced great difficulty in performing even simple tasks, but after a week the inverted world appeared reasonably normal and he was able to get about with comparative ease – he had 'adapted'.

In another experiment Stratton built an optical arrangement which visually displaced his own body so that he always appeared horizontally in front of himself. He wore this system continually and after three days he was able to go out for walks.

There have been many similar experiments in which the visual world has been rearranged. All the reports suggest that people can adjust or adapt: they learn to reach for objects in the correct place in the new visual world, and after a period they can perform tasks more or less normally.

In Stratton's experiment (*above*) the mirror arrangement allowed the wearer to see himself suspended in space.
Snyder and Pronko's lens system (*right*) inverts and displaces the visual world.

Upside-down and reversed left to right worlds

Snyder and Pronko have reported some experiments on subjects using a lens system which inverted the world and also reversed it from left to right, and vice versa. Not only did objects appear upside-down, but those on the right of the subject appeared on his left, and vice versa. (In psychology a person who is experimented upon is usually called a subject.) The inverting goggles were worn continually for thirty days. Again the subjects learned to adapt to this bizarre world. One hair-raising account was reported by a subject who had gone for a car ride. He was able to adjust to upside-down cars appearing from the wrong side of the road, but could never adjust to the fact that the sound of them appeared from the opposite side.

The process that Stratton and later Pronko and Snyder studied is called *perceptual adaptation*. The usual way to study this phenomenon in the psychological laboratory is to use a device – usually a prism – which transforms the visual world (inverting it, for example) and then to observe how subjects learn to adapt. A subject is said to have adapted if his performance on various tasks matches his pre-experimental performance.

If a subject wears goggles fitted with wedge prisms he experiences a sideways displacement of everything in his visual environment. The light passing through the prism is displaced in the direction of the base, so the apparent direction of the object is shifted in the direction of the apex of the prism. Most of the recent work on perceptual adaptation has been done using wedge prisms.

The psychologist is interested in two main questions with respect to adaptation to transformed visual inputs – the length of time it takes adaptation to occur, and how and under what conditions it occurs.

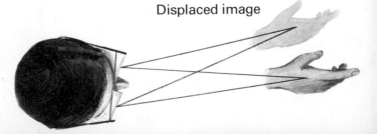

Displaced image

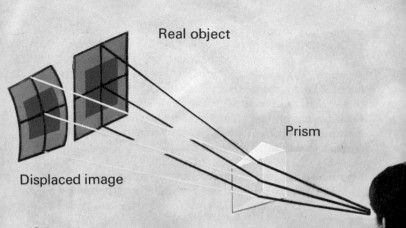

Real object

Displaced image

Prism

(*Below left*) Subjects wearing prisms adapt to a displaced visual world by correlating active movement with displacement. (*Above*) Viewed through a prism the object appears displaced to the left and bowed to the right.

Why study perceptual adaptation?

The study of adaptation has potential practical use. In deep-sea diving the diver is exposed to all kinds of distorted perceptual inputs, chiefly due to the effect of light travelling through water. One perceptual effect is that underwater objects appear magnified. If a diver is to repair something quickly, it is important to know how long it will take him to adapt, and also the best conditions under which this adaptation occurs.

Perceptual adaptation, and especially the circumstances under which it occurs, may be of special interest to a developmental psychologist. A developmental psychologist's main research interest is in the way the capabilities of humans form and grow to their adult level of competence, be it perception, language, thinking or intelligence.

The study of the way and circumstances under which adults adapt to rearrangements of the visual world might possibly be a simulation of conditions present at an earlier stage of the perceptual development of the child, and the conditions controlling adaptation could offer some answers about the possible mechanisms underlying the infant's perception of a stable world.

There remains a puzzle, however. We have already seen that there is some evidence that many perceptual processes are not learnt but innate, and it seems that they are already built into the nervous system of the newborn baby. One of these is that the infant does perceive a stable world of objects. The work on perceptual adaptation, however, suggests that the perceptual world is modifiable, and that human beings can adapt to a wide variety of visual worlds.

The conditions under which adaptation occurs

Experiments by Richard Held and his colleagues involved subjects wearing goggles with wedge prisms which distorted the physical environment so that the world appeared shifted to one side.

He found that his subjects were eventually able to adjust to this abnormal environment but there was one important proviso: the subjects only learnt to adapt if they were actively manipulating the environment, walking, reaching for objects and touching them. If they were merely passively observing the transformed visual world they never did adapt. It seemed that what was necessary for adaptations to occur was to achieve a correlation between bodily movements and the distorted visual input.

After-effects and adaptation

When an 'active' subject wearing wedge prisms views a straight line for example, it appears curved to one side, and when the goggles are removed the line appears to curve in the opposite direction. This perceptual effect is called an after-effect and it usually quickly wears off. If a 'passive' subject wears a wedge prism and views a straight line, however, it still appears to curve, but when the goggles are removed he gets no after-effect.

Held wondered if he could obtain an after-effect of a stimulus even if the subject had not viewed that particular stimulus while wearing prisms. To find out, he constructed an apparatus which consisted of a large drum on the inside surface of which was a random pattern of dots with no straight lines. This pattern looked the same whether it was viewed through a prism or not. The subjects entered the drum two at a time wearing prism goggles. One of them was active, walking around inside the drum, while the passive subject was wheeled about on a trolley. They both stayed in the drum for thirty minutes, after which they were tested for after-effects by judging a straight line. All the active subjects had an after-effect – they perceived the straight line as curved – whereas none of the passive subjects suffered this effect.

It seemed that motor movement alone had somehow altered the subjective geometry of the active subject. Indeed all of Held's experiments point to a puzzling (at the moment) connection between perception and bodily movement.

Subjects exposed to distorted visual inputs in one of Held's experiments.

Language and perception

A problem which has had a long history in philosophy concerns the relationship between language and the way the world is perceived. More recently it has been revived by the anthropologist and linguist B. J. Whorf, who has suggested that what an individual perceives is categorized and restricted by the language at his disposal. That is to say, people from different cultures perceive the world differently because of their different languages. It has been pointed out in this connection that because Eskimos have fifty different words for snow (or so it is alleged), they are able to 'see' many more kinds than a European whose vocabulary for snow is more modest. Stated in this strong form Whorf's hypothesis is clearly untenable; merely having more words cannot of itself increase perceptual discrimination. With practice a European could make as many discriminations between the different kinds of snow as the Eskimo. He might, for example, describe one type as being 'greyish – white – mottled – flaky – crystalline – snow', whereas the Eskimo might well have one word in his language for that particular kind. It seems then that the Eskimo just has a more efficient coding system to describe this significant feature of his environment than the European, who is not usually called upon to distinguish between the different types of snow.

One difficulty with the Whorfian hypothesis concerns the perceptual capabilities of very young infants. Bower showed that they acquire the conception of solidity long before they have any language competence.

Personality and perception

Whorf's hypothesis suggests that there might be differences between people from different language groups in the way they perceive the world. Is it possible that individuals from the *same* language culture perceive the world in different ways?

There is some evidence for a link between an individual's personality and his manner of perception. Witkin and his colleagues have tested children and adults in a variety of situations, and in one experiment children were placed in a room which could be rotated. The subjects sat in a 'tilted' chair, the room was rotated and they were required to adjust

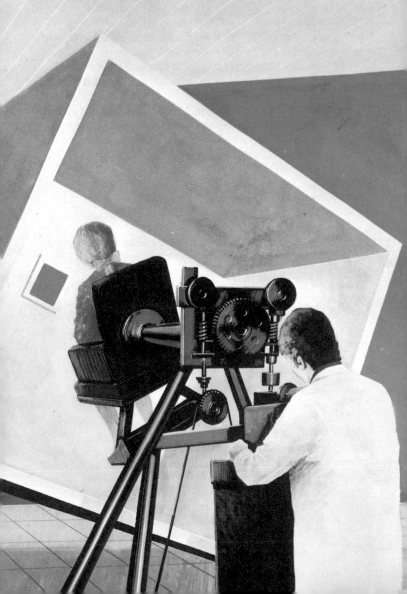

A subject seated in a tilted chair in Witkin's tilted room test.

their chair until they were sitting upright with respect to the pull of gravity. Witkin found that the ability of his subjects to do this varied, and among them were those who fell into two extreme groups. There were those who were able to do this very easily, and these subjects were called *field-independent*; and there were those who were unable to perform this task, and these were called *field-dependent*.

Witkin also found this field 'dependence–independence' dimension in other tasks. In his rod-and-frame test where subjects were called upon to make a judgement similar to that made in the rotating room test, children or adults sat in a room which was pitch dark except for a luminous square frame hanging on a wall near to the subject. The vertical frame could be rotated by the experimenter and brought to rest at any angle to the horizontal. Within this frame was a luminous rod which could be rotated by the subject. The rod was initially placed at an angle away from the true vertical, and each subject was required to adjust the rod to this direction.

Although the field-independent subjects were able to perform this task successfully, the field-dependent subjects were unable to align the luminous rod to the vertical. They appeared to be distracted by the square frame which had been rotated at an angle to the horizontal. The walls of the room were not visible and so the field-dependent subjects could only rely on the luminous frame for visual clues to the vertical, and this gave false ones. It seemed that the field-dependent subjects were unable to suppress these false background cues in making their judgements.

Embedded figure tests

Witkin has also found that field-independent adults and children similarly tended to do better on the 'embedded figure tests' than the field-dependent subjects. Embedded figure tests camouflage simple figures by having them placed in more complex designs, and subjects are required to locate a simple pattern embedded in a more complicated one. In these tests, the more analytical field-independent individuals are less hindered by the conflicting background cues of the complex design than the field-dependent subjects.

Witkin has suggested that these 'visual types', the field-

The figures on the left are camouflaged in those on the right in the embedded figured tests.

17

dependent and field-independent subjects, can be correlated with two personality types. The field-dependent person is supposed to rely exclusively on his social environment for emotional security, and he tends to take a global approach to his perceptual and intellectual tasks. The field-independent person is supposed to be socially independent and to be more analytical in his perception; that is to say, he can make more discriminations because he is less global in his approach to the world.

Cognitive styles and perception

The work of Witkin seems to show that there are differences between individuals in the way they handle the information at their disposal. These differences are usually referred to as *cognitive* (sometimes *intellectual*) *styles* and they are linked with the habitual ways individuals have of dealing with information – whether it be visual or intellectual – about one's self or one's environment.

Another interesting example of a cognitive style is the levellers–sharpeners dimension studied by Holzman and

The cards used in Holzman and Klein's 'cat and dog' experiment.

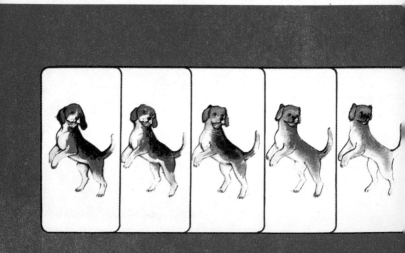

Klein. Again their research showed the existence of two extreme groups of individuals on opposite ends of this dimension. Levellers always tended to minimize differences between stimuli or intellectual concepts. Sharpeners were those who habitually preserved or accentuated the differences in the stimuli.

A typical test situation was as follows: a series of similar stimuli which gradually changed in (say) length was presented to each of these two groups of subjects. The sharpeners always perceived the stimulus change very accurately whereas the levellers did not; they were prone to give the same size estimate all through the gradually changing set of stimuli.

One rather spectacular example of this cognitive style was in the 'cat and dog' experiment conducted on subjects who had previously been diagnosed as either a leveller or a sharpener. Each person was presented with a series of cards on each of which was a picture. The first picture quite plainly showed a dog and the last one a cat. Each of the intervening pictures exhibited a gradual transition from the dog into the cat in discrete changes. The sharpeners immediately recognized that the stimulus was changing into a cat, but some of the levellers persisted in their judgement, right up to the end of the series, that the picture showed a dog.

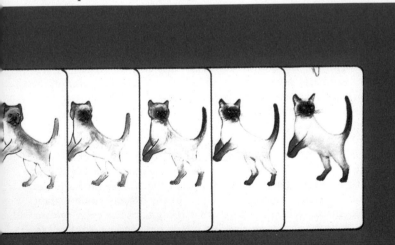

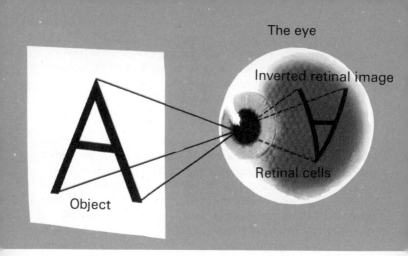

The eye

Inverted retinal image

Retinal cells

Object

A possible template theory of pattern recognition. (*Above*) The figure as perceived by the eye and (*opposite*) as relayed to the brain.

Visual pattern recognition

The goal of psychologists interested in perception (the process of becoming aware of objects by sound, feel or sight, by way of the ears, touch or the eyes), is to understand the psychological processes that operate when we recognize objects, read the letters on a page, or listen to speech. The brain is somehow able to convert the visual symbols on a page to meaningful phrases, and the spoken words to meaningful sentences.

Pattern recognition – it would have been better called object recognition – is concerned with the way external signals arrive at the sense organs to be converted into meaningful perceptual experiences. In this section we shall consider only visual pattern recognition – the way the brain recognizes objects that are presented to the eye.

The eye is often likened to a simple camera and the implication of this is that the image on the retina is an exact copy of the perceived object, so that the brain simply reacts to the retinal image. This further supposes that the brain harbours an exact three-dimensional 'copy' of the object which is then recognized. What is it then, that recognizes the copy within the brain? Another mechanism would have to be postulated to recognize this internal copy.

Template matching theories

Template matching theories of pattern recognition assume that each time an object, a face, or a letter A for instance, is presented for recognition, the brain searches for an already stored 'match' in memory. When this is located recognition is achieved.

If, for example, a letter A is presented to the eye its image falls on the retina exciting an A-shaped configuration of cells. Such a configuration of retinal cells, according to this type of theory, is connected to a single cell within the brain. This detector cell constitutes a template specifically designed to detect the occurrence of the letter A.

A template recognition scheme for human pattern recognition is in fact untenable. The particular configuration of receptors 'fired' at the retina depends on the size and orienta-

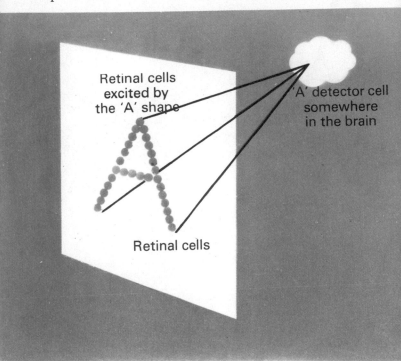

Retinal cells excited by the 'A' shape

'A' detector cell somewhere in the brain

Retinal cells

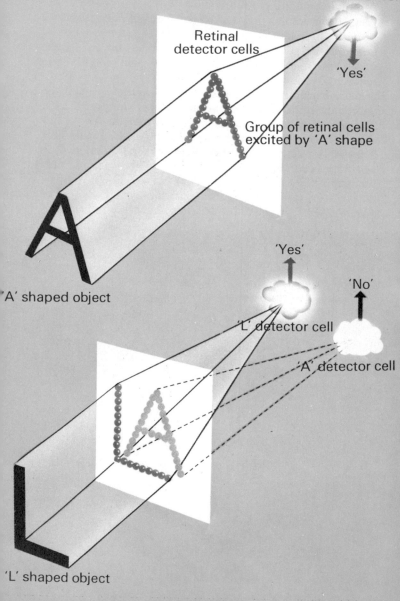

'A' detector cell

'Yes'

Retinal detector cells

Group of retinal cells excited by 'A' shape

'A' shaped object

'Yes'

'No'

'L' detector cell

'A' detector cell

'L' shaped object

tion of the object. For each different orientation or size of the letter A, a different configuration of receptors (or cells) at the retina would have to be excited. This would mean an infinite number of templates for the same object. Another difficulty with this kind of theory is that it does not account for the fact that though the retinal image of a solid object is two-dimensional, it is perceived as three-dimensional.

Feature testing theories

How are we to account for the fact that we perceive objects despite a degraded two-dimensional image at the retina? Feature testing theories of pattern recognition suggest that the brain operates not on a 'picture' on the retina – as template theories suggest – but on certain selected *features* of the input (perhaps lines, angles and movements in certain directions).

The idea is that the visual system identifies a few features of the pattern. The letter A can be thought of as consisting of the following features: two sloping lines, an acute angle and a single horizontal line. A particular pattern, then, consists of a unique set of features and the recognition process consists of tallying an inventory of features in order to arrive at the identity of the object.

The letters B and P have many features in common whereas A and B have few. Other features used in the identification of stimuli are edges and lines, and there is some neuro-physiological evidence that the brain 'extracts' particular features from patterns in order to identify them.

Interpretation

The recognition and the perception of objects in the external world is not simply a matter of a passive sensing of the environment in which images are projected on to the retina for the brain to simply register; this presupposes a 'camera' conception. Feature testing theories suggest that one does not 'see' the retinal image: one sees with the *aid* of this image. Further, the implication is that the brain reads off information from the retina in order to form hypotheses about the external

The feature testing theory of pattern recognition suggests excitation of different retinal and detector cells for different shapes.

world of objects, and this results in the conscious experience of perceiving.

In a very real sense perception and pattern recognition involve the building up of hypotheses – based on the inadequate sensory data impinging on the retina – about the nature of the external world. On this view all perceptions are hypotheses.

The Muller-Lyer illusion

The Muller-Lyer illusion consists of two equal-sized shafts. On one of them is connected a pair of reversed arrow-heads, while on the other there is attached a pair of normal heads. The illusion is that the reversed arrow-heads seem to lengthen the shaft, whereas normal arrow-heads appear to shrink the shaft.

One explanation of this illusion suggests that *size constancy* is involved – the brain appears to be able to compensate for an apparent retinal-image size decrease.

The theory proposes that if in some two-dimensional pictures (such as the Muller-Lyer illusion) there are cues which suggest distance perspective, then the brain will automatically compensate for the expected shrinkage of 'far away objects' by a misplaced size constancy adjustment.

In the Muller-Lyer illusion the shaft with the normal arrow-heads serves as perspective cues in ordinary pictures, and this line is therefore interpreted as being nearer to the perceiver than the shaft with reversed arrow-heads. This 'far away' shaft is therefore a candidate for enlargement by a misplaced size constancy adjustment – hence the illusion.

With the Muller-Lyer illusion the brain brings rules and hypotheses to bear in the perception of a two-dimensional picture derived from experience gained in the real three-dimensional world. Sensory evidence falling on the retina must be *interpreted* by the brain according to rules or hypotheses. The brain reads off certain selected features of the input, probably lines, edges and angles. From this rather meagre information it interprets the nature of the object and constructs an internal brain model.

The shaft in the bottom figure *appears* longer than the shaft above it in the Muller-Lyer illusion.

Rules and hypotheses for finding objects in two-dimensional scenes

Sensory evidence falling on the retina must be interpreted by the brain and the strong implication is that there must be rules which the brain uses to accomplish this.

A look at the illustration on this page will help to focus some questions. The immediate perception is of a pair of three-dimensional objects: a cube overlapping the wedge. Why are two objects seen instead of one? How, in fact, do we perceive the three surfaces as a cube in front of a wedge with two surfaces? How is it known that the areas b and c come from the same object, but areas d and e come from different objects? Again, how does this two-dimensional picture convey an impression of a pair of three-dimensional objects?

These questions are so simple and fundamental that we hardly ever ask ourselves them. It is this obviousness that makes such questions so difficult to answer. It must be, however, that the brain uses rules and hypotheses to dissect such

A two-dimensional scene: a cube overlapping a wedge.

scenes into objects, here a wedge and a cube.

Guzman, a computer scientist working in artificial intelligence research, has written a program called SEE which nicely exemplifies the problems involved in this seemingly simple task.

First a series of programs were made to operate directly on the two-dimensional scene. Their job was to locate geometric features of the picture: regions, edges and vertices into types: the most important were *arrows*, *forks* and *tees*.

If the vertex forms a fork usually all three surfaces belong to the same object: d, e and f. An arrow usually signifies two objects, one that contains surfaces h and i, and the other containing j. A tee often means that one object is in front of another, so that generally surfaces k and l belong to one object that passes in front of another object that has a surface m.

To illustrate how the SEE program dissects a picture into separate objects an example will be given as to how this is done for the cube and wedge.

Types of vertices that can provide cues for dissecting scenes into separate objects.

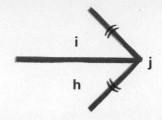

Arrow. Three lines meet at a point separating i, j and h, with one angle greater than 180°.

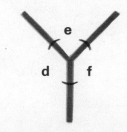

Fork. Three lines forming angles smaller than 180°; these three lines separate regions d, e and f.

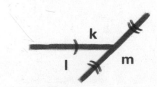

Tee. Three concurrent lines, two of which are colinear, separating three regions k, l and m.

Cues for object dissection:
(separates faces of the same object,
((separates faces of different objects.

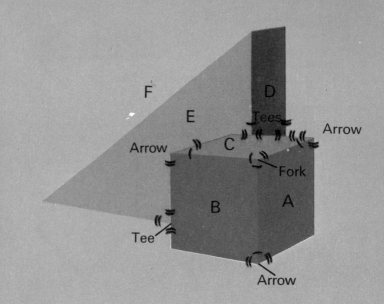

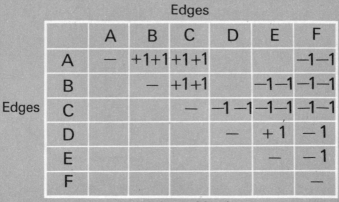

Edges

	A	B	C	D	E	F
A	—	+1+1	+1+1			−1−1
B		—	+1+1		−1−1	−1−1
C			—	−1−1	−1−1	−1−1
D				—	+1	−1
E					—	−1
F						—

Linkage Matrix

Dissecting objects from scenes

In the diagram opposite the same cube and wedge are shown but with the appropriate vertex types indicated together with a linkage table or matrix.

One rule which the program can use when it scans each of the vertices is: if the edges are likely to separate faces of the same object they are scored $+1$; edges that are likely to separate faces of different objects are scored -1.

First consider the fork vertices (there is only one). Surface A has positive links to both B and C, so a $+1$ is entered for each in the linkage matrix.

Now consider the three arrow vertices. For arrow 1, surface A has positive links to surface C, so a $+1$ is scored in the linkage matrix, whereas both A and C have negative links to F, so -1 is scored for each of them respectively. This procedure is followed for arrows 2 and 3.

Next examine the three tee vertices; each time the edges separate faces of the same object score $+1$, and -1 if they do not. Guzman's program then examines the completed linkage matrix. All those surfaces which have a tie of $+1$ to each other are treated as one object. From this, it can be seen that the picture is dissected into two objects ABC and DE – the cube and wedge respectively.

Computer theories and brain theories

What does Guzman's program show? It suggests that the brain may work on two different levels when analysing two-dimensional scenes, and probably in any object recognition task. There is first an initial extraction of features – in the SEE program an examination of different types of vertices – and simultaneously there is an interpretation process to find out the possible meanings conveyed by those features. This interpretation is aided by the use of rules or hypotheses, and some possible ones have already been indicated. For instance, if the program detects a fork in the scene the hypothesis is: 'probably all three surfaces belong to the same object'.

Guzman's work points to a possible theory of human pattern recognition: the camera or template analogy is a mistaken one;

How the SEE program dissects objects from scenes.

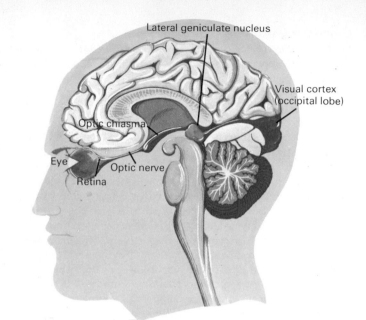

Side view of visual system.

perceived objects cannot be described as faithful pictures on the retina which the brain projects wholesale into the back of the mind to give the conscious experience of perception.

Rather the suggestion is: the brain extracts only a few selected features of the image on the retina; on the basis of these features, however, it constructs an internal brain model of the object by the use of hypotheses and inferences.

The brain and eye

The brains of human beings are symmetrical. We have two arms, two legs, two eyes, two ears and two 'brains', or rather two hemispheres, the left and right hemisphere.

When we study an object with our eyes it undergoes a reversal at the retina. That is to say, light rays intersect at the lens of the eye so as to project a reversed image on the retina. From there nerve impulses travel along a bundle of nerve fibres – the visual pathways. These visual pathways from the retina to the brain make up what is called the optic nerve.

Images falling on the inside (nasal) half of each retina are projected via the optic nerve fibres to the opposite side of the brain, while images on the outside half of each retina are projected on to the same side of the brain. This system provides us with overlapping binocular vision.

The optic nerve fibres from the outer half of each retina do not cross over from one hemisphere to the other, but those from the inside half of each retina do, and they cross over at a point in the brain called the *optic chiasma*.

If a cut is made through the middle of the optic chiasma the left hemisphere receives information only from the left eye, while the right hemisphere receives information only from the right eye.

The eye is an organ which consists essentially of structures to ensure that light falls on the retina. To enable the retina to transform the sensory input into nerve impulses, use is made of three distinct types of retinal cells or neurones: the rods and cones, bipolar cells and ganglion cells. The rods and cones are light detectors; these transmit information to the bipolar cells which in turn transmit information to the ganglion cells which form the optic nerve.

Plan view of visual system.

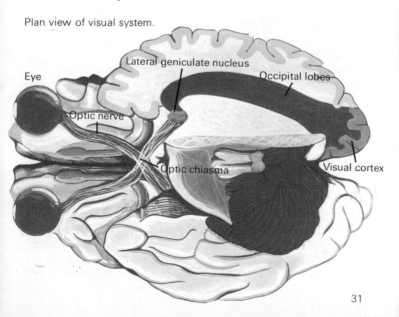

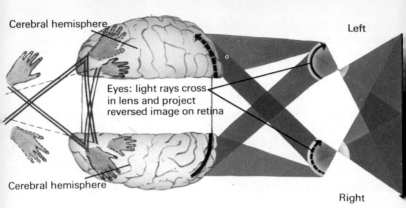

Viewed objects undergo a reversal at the retina, each half appearing on *opposite* sides of the brain.

Signals that leave the retina travel along the optic nerve until they arrive at the lateral geniculate nucleus. Here the long nerve fibres from the retinal cells make connections with new cells that will carry information to the cortical receiving areas.

Feature detection in the brain

Computer theories of pattern recognition suggest that the brain operates not on a 'picture' on the retina, but on certain selected features of the input, perhaps lines, angles and movement. This might lead us to suppose that somewhere in the visual system there are cells or neurones which are designed to detect particular features of the input. In animal visual systems this has certainly been found to be true. Neurophysiologists have found that certain patterns at the eye produce activity in specific cells of the brain. A line, for instance, moving in a particular direction produces activity in some cells but not in others, while movement of the same line in the opposite direction will activate an altogether different set of cells.

Hubel and Wiesel have discovered a number of features of retinal patterns which are extracted by the brain – at least of the cat. They have found cells in the visual cortex of the cat which respond only to edges of a particular orientation. All the neurophysiological work done so far to locate cells in the brain which fire to specific features of the retinal image have been done on animals, but it is very probable that the human brain is also endowed with specific feature detection cells.

The work of the neurophysiologists has a number of implications. One is that the existence of feature detection systems points to the conclusion that a great deal of perception must be innate; the nervous system seems to be specially built to extract particular features of the input. It is equally probable that experience plays a part in developing the detector cells.

The brain is so complex and bewildering that it is impossible to study it in isolation; in fact we must study the brain with pre-conceived notions or hypotheses, and to do this we compare it with devices or 'models' we already know a lot about. The model increasingly used by psychologists to explain brain functions is the computer. In this way, computer theories and psychological experiments will tell the neurophysiologists what to look for in their search to understand how the brain perceives the world.

Crossover of information occurs along the optic chiasma.

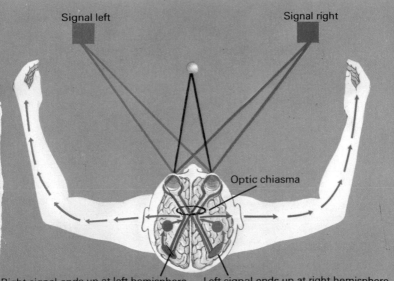

MEMORY

Memory, like all psychological phenomena, has two facets: an internal introspective and an external observable one. All of us have memories which retain vivid, atmospheric intangible sensations which are inaccessible to anyone but us. These can be recalled and recounted to another person, but what we present is only an external picture. Some of the descriptions of places and events can be verified by a listener, but the two participants will have access to very different aspects of this phenomenon called memory. No matter how well observable behaviour stands up to objective tests, an external observer or experimenter cannot observe or verify what we claim to have *experienced* in memory.

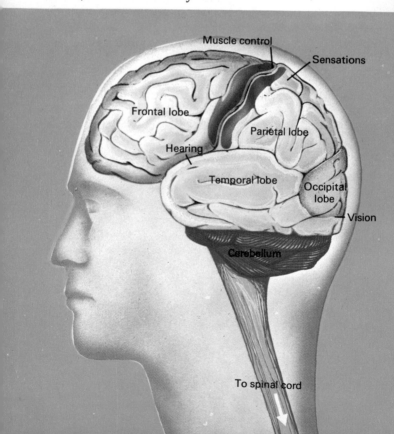

The brain and memory

Viewed from above the brain appears as two hemispheres which together form the cerebral cortex. The different sections of the cortex have been given names. The front parts are called the frontal lobes, on the sides are the parietal lobes and the temporal lobes, and to the rear are the occipital lobes.

The brain has 10,000 million brain cells or neurones which are interconnected, creating a structure of amazing complexity. Men and animals are affected by their experiences which, it is certain, produce changes in the brain.

Scientists working on the brain/memory problem have asked three basic questions. First, when do these changes occur? Second, what is the nature of these changes? Third, where in the brain are these changes likely to happen?

All our knowledge of memory comes from observing external events: usually by observing what people say and do, or investigating physical and chemical changes in the brain tissue. Work on memory aims to understand the mechanisms which in human beings mediate the experience of memory, and herein lies a difficult paradox. Our intuitions – perhaps mistakenly – tell us that there exists a separate class of events, mental events, which cannot be described in terms of the concepts employed by the physical sciences. Yet the hope is, again perhaps mistakenly, that an account of mind, experience and consciousness can be obtained by investigating the brain in terms of the same concepts used to study inanimate objects found in the rest of nature.

When do these changes occur in the brain?

Head injury caused by a severe blow or a car accident can disrupt memory. A common form of amnesia (loss of memory) brought about by such injury, or an electric shock delivered to the head, is retrograde amnesia (RA), which is a loss of memory for events prior to the accident. The period of RA (which may be months or even years), gradually shrinks, but studies on patients who have suffered this type of memory loss show that the memory for events that occurred a few moments before the accident seems to be lost forever.

Some of the brain structures involved in sensation and memory.

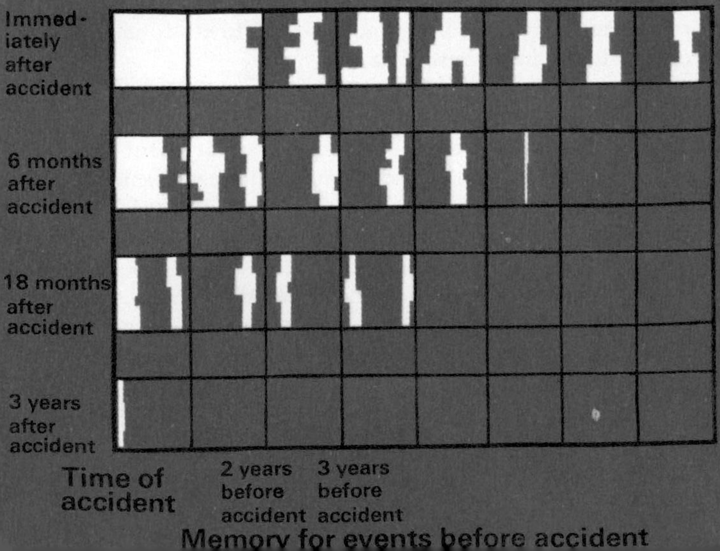

Immediately after accident

6 months after accident

18 months after accident

3 years after accident

Time of accident · 2 years before accident · 3 years before accident

Memory for events before accident

Electroconvulsive shock (ECS), used for the treatment of some psychiatric disorders, consists of the application of an electric current to the brain causing convulsions, unconsciousness and loss of memory for events immediately preceding the convulsion.

These observations together with the fact that it is only very recent memories which are permanently erased, leaving the older ones relatively intact, has led Hebb and other investigators to suggest the *consolidation theory of memory*. This proposes that memory is a two-stage process. The first stage consists of transient electrical events in the brain which are easily disrupted, and is identified with a short term or immediate memory. The second assumes that the initial electrical events somehow produce a more durable structural change – and more resistant to disruption – which underlies the permanent or long-term memory.

The effects of head injury or electric shock to the brain suggest that there are at least two memory systems, one for short-term storage and the other for long-term. A short-term memory system is consistent with experience, we remember events that have just happened for a brief period, and few of these need to be permanently stored and remembered.

If the brain sustains either a blow or shock, the mechanism which converts the short-term electrical events into a more permanent record is disrupted, so preventing access of experiences into the long-term memory.

The nature of the changes in the brain

What sort of changes take place in the brain when something is learned and therefore laid down in long-term memory?

One theory now no longer taken seriously is that permanent memory is mediated by some form of electrical storage. The idea was that each stored experience is represented by a particular electrical configuration in the brain – rather like a template – which if activated gives rise to consciousness of the event. However, ECS disrupts short-term memory but not permanent memory.

Course of memory loss due to retrograde amnesia following an accident. The light parts represent total memory loss.

1. Hungry dog sees food and starts eating. **2.** Dog is reprimanded whilst still eating. **3.** Dog is still hungry. **4.** Dog returns to food. **5.** Dog remembers former punishment when last eating food. **6.** Another hungry dog sees food. **7.** This dog is also reprimanded

The general opinion now is that the neural basis of permanent memory must be due to chemical changes in the brain. This poses two questions. First, how do the initial electrical events underlying short-term memory become translated into the biochemical changes for permanent storage? Second, what is the nature of this biochemical change?

There are no answers to the first question and there are only

whilst eating. **8.** Dog is subjected to electro-convulsive shock and forgets events immediately prior to treatment. **9.** Treated dog, still hungry, sees food but has forgotten punishment. **10.** Treated dog eats happily, despite presence of punisher.

clues to the second. One was provided by Bennett, Diamond, Krech and Rosenzweig. They reported an experiment which showed that different environmental experiences produced differences in the brain chemistry of rats. They found that rats reared in stimulating environments developed a thicker and heavier cerebral cortex than rats reared in surroundings which were unstimulating.

Where the changes occur in the brain

Most of the clues about possible memory storage locations again come from observations of patients with head injury. Patients suffering from a damaged hippocampus (a structure deep in the brain), are unable to remember new information for more than a few seconds. These patients seem to have both an intact short-term memory and a long-term memory as they are able to speak. This means that they can draw on long-term memory for words, but the mechanism responsible for access to the long-term store from immediate memory, does not appear to work. Much new information about long-term storage has come from the work on 'split brains' by Sperry and his colleagues.

Split-brain studies

The human brain and most animal brains comprise two hemispheres joined by a thick bundle of nerve fibres, the *corpus callosum*. If this is cut, disconnecting the two hemispheres, the result is called a split brain.

The optic fibres from the eye to the brain intersect at the

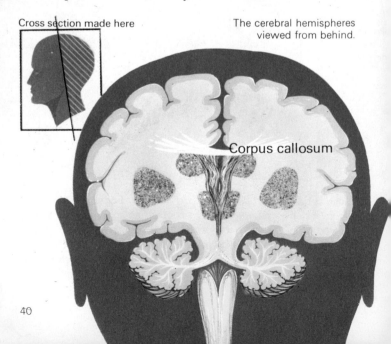

Cross section made here

The cerebral hemispheres viewed from behind.

Corpus callosum

optic chiasma (see page 31), and if a cut is made through this structure each eye can relay information only to the hemisphere on the same side of the head.

Myers, a colleague of Sperry, cut the chiasma of a cat and trained it to do a task with the left eye opened and right eye covered. After the task was learned the animal was tested on the same task with the left eye covered and right eye open. The cat successfully performed the task even though the right hemisphere had no direct previous experience with the information. It seemed that whatever is stored in one hemisphere can be transferred to the other.

Myers then prepared a split-brain cat by cutting the corpus callosum and chiasma. Again one eye was covered and the animal was trained with the other eye opened. After training, the other eye was covered and the cat was tested on the task with the previously closed eye open. The cat was unable to perform the task. This result showed that the corpus callosum provides the communication channel which allows transfer of memory and learning from one hemisphere to the other.

It would also appear that split-brain animals with a severed

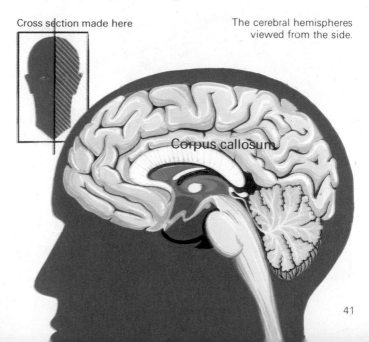

Cross section made here

The cerebral hemispheres viewed from the side.

Corpus callosum

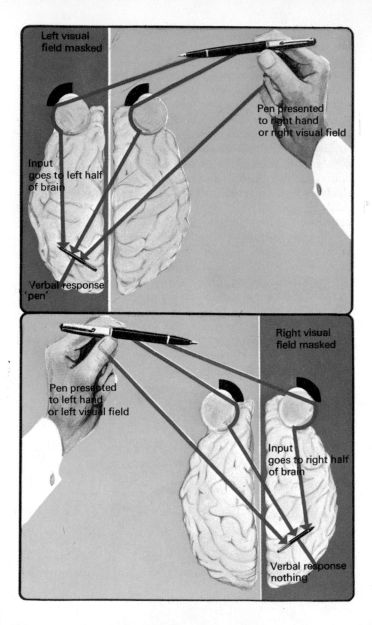

Left visual field masked

Pen presented to right hand or right visual field

Input goes to left half of brain

Verbal response 'pen'

Pen presented to left hand or left visual field

Right visual field masked

Input goes to right half of brain

Verbal response 'nothing'

chiasma seem to literally have two brains. The hemispheres can be taught contradictory responses to the same stimulus.

Split-brains in humans

Patients undergoing surgical cutting of the corpus callosum submit to the operation known as commissorotomy. This can prevent the spread of epileptic seizures from one hemisphere to the other.

The effect of cutting the corpus callosum is to prevent the transfer of events recorded in one hemisphere into the other, but patients who have undergone such an operation seem to suffer from no ill-effects. This is because each of the eyes project the same information to both hemispheres. Wide differences between these patients and normal people can be detected, however, if they submit to special testing procedures. In essence these tests restrict the sensory input to a single hemisphere of the brain, and if questions are asked about the input it is possible to evaluate the memory capabilities of each of the hemispheres.

When an object is presented to the right half of the visual field it stimulates the left portion of the two retinas and the object is projected into the left hemisphere. In the same way an object presented from the left visual field gets projected into the right hemisphere. When an object is presented in the right visual field, so that it ends up in the left half of the brain, the patient can name and describe the object. If an object is presented from the left half of the visual field, however – so that the object ends up in the right hemisphere – the patient is unable to make a verbal response and he cannot name the object. This is because although the right hemisphere becomes aware of the object, it does not control the speech mechanisms of the brain. Meanwhile, because the corpus callosum is cut, the left hemisphere controlling the speech mechanism remains unaware of the stimulus relayed to the brain's right half.

Similar experiments show that the two hemispheres of the human brain serve different functions. The left hemisphere controls language, reading and symbolic functions, and the 'speechless' hemisphere dominates in non-verbal functions.

The functions of the two hemispheres of the brain.

LEARNING

It is the view of most psychologists that much of everyday behaviour has come about as a result of learning. This is true not only of the facts we know such as our name, address and multiplication tables, but also of our attitudes, motives and personality.

These qualities are to a great extent products of socialization. Socialization refers to the process whereby individuals learn and develop those abilities which enable them to function effectively in a community. The newborn child has to be inducted into a society: it must learn the language of the culture, the appropriate behaviour of its sex, and it has to learn to value social approval in order that it will adopt socially accepted behaviours, and relinquish those deemed antisocial.

Behaviourism

Psychologists have long been trying to understand the nature of the phenomenon of learning, and among the first who seriously set out to do this were the 'behaviourist' psychologists. The word behaviourism is widely misunderstood, and this is partly because there are so many different varieties. One belief they all share, however, is that the rules of procedure for gathering evidence and data in psychological experiments should be the same as those for other sciences.

Before the behaviourist movement the subject matter for the study of human beings was images, dreams and other denizens of conscious and unconscious experience, and the early psychologists had to rely on their subjects' introspective reports and descriptions as to these mental events. The main behaviourist criticism of this procedure was that the subject matter of these experiments was not visible for public inspection, that is, to an outside objective observer.

These and similar strictures had the effect of changing the type of events that psychologists studied in an experiment, and in place of internal mental events, they observed only those events which were public and therefore external to the subject's mind: the stimulus impinging on him and his response to it, and all references to what he felt or experienced during the experiment, were suppressed.

J. B. Watson, the American behaviourist.

Ivan Pavlov, the Russian physiologist.

Although all behaviourists shared the same rules of procedure as to what kinds of data were collected and how, they nevertheless differed among themselves in many important ways. John Watson initiated one version of behaviourism which, in a more developed and sophisticated form, today represents an important and influential movement in psychology associated with the name of B. F. Skinner.

Watson took an extreme environmentalist standpoint, that is, a belief that attitudes, intellectual ability and personality are completely determined by learning as a result of environmental experiences; and an individual's genetic endowment has no effect on the development of these attributes.

Psychological theories of learning

Modern behaviourists and experimental psychologists, despite their differences in approach to the study of behaviour, take just one of two distinct points of departure in their explanation of human learning. The first of these sets out a path followed by Watson, Pavlov and Skinner, and the modern behaviourists. Learning is seen as the establishing of habits which are formed as a result of an association between a stimulus in the environment and a subject's response to it.

An example of this type of learning is the naming of objects. An Englishman learning French might have an animal, a cat

Apparatus used by Pavlov to study classical conditioning in dogs.

for example, pointed out to him. This acts as a stimulus for the associated response 'le chat'. When the French word has been mastered and the connection between the stimulus and response established, then a verbal habit has been formed. Modern behaviourists believe that all learned behaviour can be explained in terms of habit formation, and they use these rather simple concepts to explain how human beings acquire language and attitudes.

Other psychologists also working in the experimental tradition are more impressed by the role of thinking, understanding, memory and other cognitive processes in learning than by habit formations. Cognitive processes are concerned with how the brain deals with incoming stimuli in order that a response can be made, but since these processes go on inside the head, they are largely ignored by behaviourists.

Associative learning: classical conditioning

One type of associative learning – classical conditioning – was discovered by Ivan Pavlov. Most of Pavlov's classical conditioning experiments were carried out on dogs harnessed to a special apparatus, and the amount of salivation elicited during an experiment measured.

When a hungry untrained dog is first placed in the apparatus it does not salivate when a light is switched on. Normally, it only salivates after it has tasted food. This connection between the dog's response (salivation), to the taste of meat (the stimulus) is unlearned and probably innate.

In one experiment Pavlov presented a light stimulus to a dog, followed quickly by food which the dog ate, and the amount of salivation was recorded. More identical trials followed; Pavlov found that after a number of such trials the light stimulus – though previously inadequate – was sufficient to produce a salivation response. The dog had become conditioned.

Classical conditioning is an example of associative learning, a response (salivation) has become connected (conditioned) to a stimulus (the light), where previously no such association existed. Pavlov called the natural adequate stimulus (the taste of food) for eliciting a response (salivation) *the unconditioned stimulus*, and its natural response the *unconditioned response*.

1	BELL ⟶ CS (conditioned stimulus)	NO RESPONSE IN UNCONDITIONED DOG
2	FOOD ⟶ UCS (unconditioned stimulus)	SALIVARY RESPONSE IN DOG UCR (unconditioned response)
3	FOOD + BELL ⟶ UCS CS	SALIVARY RESPONSE IN DOG UCR
4	BELL ⟶ CS	SALIVARY RESPONSE IN DOG CR (conditioned response)

Classical or Pavlovian conditioning.

When learning has taken place and an association made between the light stimulus and the salivary response, they are referred to respectively as the *conditioned stimulus* and the *conditioned response*.

Associative learning: operant conditioning

Professor Skinner has concentrated almost exclusively on identifying those events in the environment, both past and present, which affect the current behaviour of an organism. Skinner's ambition is no less than to give a behaviourist account which will enable him to predict exactly how an animal or an individual will respond in any given situation. It is his claim that given a knowledge of the genetic endowment and all the stimuli impinging on a subject, it is in principle possible to predict future behaviour.

In practice the number of stimuli, and the other factors in the life history of the organism, are so vast that it is too complex an undertaking to identify the exact variables controlling the behaviour. In Skinner's view this does not mean that it is unpredictable, however. In a complicated natural environment the investigator will almost certainly overlook relevant factors

Operant conditioning. The pigeon is rewarded with food (reinforcement) each time it makes the correct response.

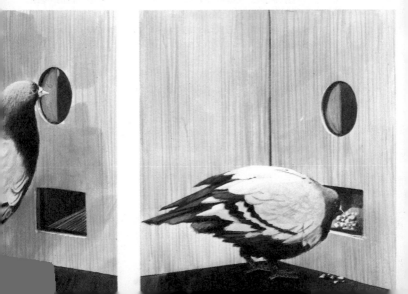

Rat in a Skinner box.

when attempting to predict behaviour, so resort is made to controlled surroundings. In a laboratory conditions can be arranged which will enable the experimenter to specify more clearly which stimuli are involved.

The idea is that under controlled conditions the environment can be altered in specifiable ways, so that certain kinds of behaviour emerge and others disappear. One piece of laboratory equipment often used for these endeavours is the Skinner box.

A Skinner box consitutes a controlled environment and it has a lever inside which, if pressed, releases a pellet of food. When an untrained hungry rat first enters the box it moves around exploring in a random fashion. This behaviour is not really random: an omniscient observer with an inventory of the animal's genetic endowment, past history, and presently available stimuli impinging on it, could predict exactly – according to Skinner – the rat's behaviour.

The rat, during its random exploring, 'accidentally' pulls the lever, releasing the food which it then eats. Unidentified stimuli in the box are responsible for the bar-pressing and the problem is, for Skinner, to get the bar-pressing response associated with the sight of the lever, and 'unhooked' from the unidentified stimuli which initially elicited the response. The food pellets are rewarding (reinforcing) and this encourages the hungry rat to stay near the lever and to the stimuli, which originally initiated the bar pressing; and so inevitably the rat again presses the bar. Gradually the lever becomes associated with the bar-pressing response. This is another example of associative learning; the lever stimulus which was not previously associated with the bar-pressing response has now become associated.

Skinner referred to this sort of learning as instrumental conditioning: this is behaviour which operates on the environment so as to produce an outcome.

Respondent and operant behaviour

Skinner distinguishes between respondent and operant behaviour. Respondent behaviour is directly under the control of a stimulus which can be explicitly identified by an observer. Operant behaviour is no less under the control of environmental stimuli, but as yet these are not identifiable.

The behaviour of an untrained rat in the Skinner box is an example of operant behaviour: it operates on the environment, evaluating the outcome, and when the rat finally learns to press the lever for food this now becomes respondent behaviour because the stimulus which controls and initiates the bar-pressing can now be precisely identified.

Reinforcement and shaping behaviour

Skinner's learning theory relies almost entirely on the law of reinforcement which states: *actions which are immediately followed by rewards (reinforcement) are repeated and learned whereas actions or behaviour which are not followed by reinforcement are dropped.*

He has been notably successful in teaching animals – usually rats and pigeons – activities which nobody previously had thought possible for them to learn, using a technique known as shaping.

Here the experimenter first decides on the sequence of movements he wants the animal to learn. As soon as the pigeon makes a movement even remotely in line with the first movement of the desired sequence, it is rewarded with a few grains of corn. Gradually this movement will become more frequent and more precise until it is reproduced perfectly, and then the next step in the sequence is shaped.

The shaping technique has been successfully used with human subjects. Fuller has reported its use with mentally subnormal patients who were unable to learn anything and were even incapable of dressing and feeding themselves.

Classical and operant conditioning

In classical or Pavlovian conditioning the reinforcement (food in our discussion) is paired with the presentation of the unconditioned stimulus (the light). In operant or instrumental conditioning reinforcement always follows the occurrence of the desired response. That is, the reinforcement is contingent upon the correct response.

Application of learning theory to human problems

Since the Second World War two major movements have emerged which attempt to deal with human problems from the standpoint of behaviourism: behaviour therapy and behaviour technology.

Behaviour therapy

Most explanations of mental illness are based on a disease concept according to which abnormalities in behaviour are considered to result from internal events, such as conflicts and other subjective states. An important method of treatment which assumes the traditional disease concept of behaviour disorders is psychoanalysis.

A very different conception favoured by behaviourist psychologists and behaviour therapists is that the symptoms of mental illness, which issue as behaviour departing widely from socially acceptable conduct, should not be regarded as evidence of an illness or disease, but as a way in which the individual has learned to cope with external circumstances. Treatment of mental illness according to the behaviour therapist then becomes a problem in social learning. Behaviour therapy refers to treatment of behaviour disorders by the use of principles derived from learning theory principally from the work of Pavlov and Skinner. Behaviour therapists typically use Pavlovian conditioning or operant conditioning methods, whichever seem to be the most appropriate for the particular patient.

If the therapist uses operant conditioning as a method of treatment, three conditions are usually met. First, the patient

Shaping behaviour. Any response of the pigeon *towards* the desired response is rewarded.

1. Specialized attention shown by a teacher to withdrawn child is undesirable. **2.** The time to exercise attention is now, when the withdrawn child joins the group. **3.** Lack of attention in the group

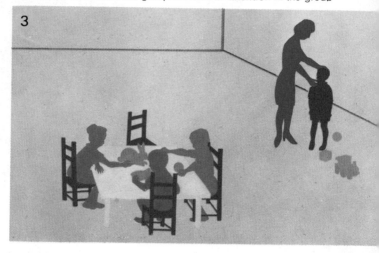

is given tangible rewards or reinforcement, praise, attention, or perhaps cigarettes or money. Second, reinforcement is always given subject to the occurrence of the desired behaviour. Third, shaping is used so that even very small improvements in the direction of the desired behaviour are rewarded.

Harris, Wolf and Baer reported an investigation where

situation causes a reversion to withdrawn state. **4.** Teacher now ignores solitary behaviour, but rewards moves towards group. Child finds group rewarding in itself.

operant conditioning techniques were used to treat abnormal behaviour in children. In one study an extremely withdrawn child, who spent most of his time in solitary activity, was treated with the aim of getting him to mix normally with other children. The therapist had noticed that the teacher unwittingly reinforced the undesired solitary behaviour by constantly paying attention to the child, in an effort to encourage him to play with other children. When the child did happen to join the others this was not usually rewarded as the teacher took no further notice of him.

The therapist remedied the situation by instructing the teacher to stop rewarding the solitary play with attention, but instead to give full attention whenever he made any move to seek out other children. In this way the solitary behaviour was eliminated and the desired behaviour rewarded by the teacher until the child at last found the company of other children rewarding in itself.

Behaviour technology

Behaviour technology refers to the direct application of operant conditioning techniques for social control, and as such it will probably come to be increasingly used in schools, hospitals, and prisons – anywhere, in fact, where behaviour is thought to be in need of modification.

Behaviour technology is motivated by the Skinnerian belief that human actions are largely regulated by their own environmental consequences, and the principle mechanism by which a change in behaviour can be wrought is through positive reinforcement.

One technique used to institute behaviour modification is the *token economy system*. The token economy had its origins in animal experiments in which chimpanzees showed they could learn to place a poker chip in a slot machine to obtain grapes, to press a bar to obtain these chips, and to save up a specified number to exchange for grapes.

This system has now been used in schools. Children who have reading difficulties due to poor motivation can be taught to read in a shorter time if their reward is a set of tokens, which they can exchange for sweets or anything else they find rewarding.

Behaviour technology bespeaks an optimistic philosophy: school children fail not because of anything 'bad' within them, but because of poor schools which fail to provide the environments for 'successful' behaviour to emerge. The mentally ill and others similarly stigmatized are not in the thralls of inner conflicts, but are victims of faulty environments which can be remedied by a piece of behavioural engineering.

A teaching machine using many of the principles of Skinner's learning theory such as reinforcement and shaping.

The achievement of Skinner

It does seem that Skinner is more interested in the control of behaviour than in understanding it. Secondly, on Skinner's scheme it is very difficult to account for novelty and creativity in behaviour. Human actions according to workers in operant conditioning are controlled and tied to the stimulus conditions in the environment.

This approach to human behaviour presents difficulties when trying to account for human language ability. Language consists in the production of novelty – of sentences never before uttered – and this fact places a great strain on Skinnerian explanations which insist that language is merely a set of verbal responses under the control of environmental stimuli.

From the turn of this century psychologists have endeavoured to account for human behaviour in terms of the antecedents of each action. Two possible types of antecedent conditions have been investigated which are thought to influence present behaviour. These are an individual's genetic endowment and the history of reward and punishments and their interaction in the life of the individual.

Skinner's contribution represents a sustained effort to account for each of our actions in terms of rewards, punishments and environmental stimuli. Like Watson before him, he has probably underemphasized the role of heredity in determining our intelligence, attitudes and personality.

The mind and free-will debate

Historically, attempts to account for human actions since the time of Descartes have taken one of two forms. First there was Descartes' assumption that human beings are endowed with minds which are totally exempt from the laws of nature. This led to the belief that any explanation of human behaviour must recognize that cause and effect mechanisms (or an inventory of antecedent causes) – though effective for an understanding of physical systems – are of little use when trying to understand human actions.

The opposite assumption, held by the behaviourists, is that minds are not exempt from the laws of nature, and so an understanding of human actions can be gleaned from the same principles used to comprehend mechanical systems.

Prediction of the behaviour of these systems can be made by a cause and effect analysis, and this was translated by psychologists to mean that human behaviour should be explained by an analysis of the antecedent conditions operating on the organism.

Nowadays, the 'hiers' of Descartes' views on human actions are the existentialist philosophers. These maintain that there are no antecedent conditions, either genetic or stimulus, which determine human behaviour: all actions are the result of free decisions from within the individual, from internal feelings and states of mind which themselves have no earlier cause. This, to them, is a faith in human freedom which spurns the doctrine of determinism – the view that all events (including human actions) have external causes.

Chart showing the course and possible direction of behavioural control techniques.

	Subjects	Aims	Workers	Locations
Experimental era (1935-1960)	Animals (rats and pigeons)	To produce and understand operant behaviour	Academic psychologists	University laboratories
Applied era (1960-)	Humans (disturbed children, mental hospital patients)	Treatment of behavioural disorders	Clinical and educational psychologists	Mental hospitals, special schools
	Family groups	Treatment of educational and social problems	Psychologists, therapists, teachers	School classrooms, prisons
The future	Schools? Social groups? Countries?	Prevention of disciplinary problems and civil disturbances	Administrators, employers, governments	Mental health centres, factories

PERSONALITY

The psychologist who studies personality is engaging in an activity that all of us practise at some time or other. Whenever two strangers meet, whether socially at a party of formally at an interview, both immediately set about judging the other. Is he or she reliable, trustworthy, or stable? This continuing activity of appraising or judging one another is probably one of the most enjoyable features of social life.

To pin down an exact definition of personality is difficult but it is certainly associated with those attributes of behaviour that makes one person different from another. It has the implication too of consistency and predictability in behaviour.

Eysenck's personality theory
Hans Eysenck, a British psychologist, has proposed a theory for sorting people into different personality types. He has

Professor Hans Eysenck of the University of London.

suggested that individuals can be divided into four different categories.

First, people divide into whether they are extravert or introvert. An extravert is someone who is sociable, outgoing, and who quickly establishes personal relationships. An introvert is the opposite; he is quiet, retiring and tends to avoid undue social contact. Eysenck also categorizes all individuals as either stable or unstable. A stable person can cope with mild stress and is not easily flustered. An unstable individual is usually chronically anxious, and more often than not suffers from a mild personality disorder.

According to Eysenck then, all individuals belong, to a greater or lesser extent, to one of four possible personality types: an unstable introvert, an unstable extravert, a stable introvert, and a stable extravert.

Cattell's trait personality theory

Cattell, an American psychologist, employs many more categories than Eysenck to describe personality, and he has suggested that to do this adequately 171 are needed. Cattell's 'categories' describe personality traits. A trait is a persisting characteristic of an individual like honesty, reliability or meanness.

Cattell's personality scheme assigns to each person a score on each of the 171 traits. Thus someone who is very honest but rather mean would obtain a high 'honesty trait score', but a low 'generosity trait score'. With this scheme, it is claimed that an individual's personality can be completely described by a profile of 171 scores, one for each of Cattell's traits.

Theories of personality formation

One major concern of the personality theorist is: How many categories are necessary to give an adequate account of personality and what are they?

Another concern is to explain why an individual has a certain personality type. Why, for example, is someone a stable extravert rather than an unstable introvert?

Theories of personality formation are of three kinds: those which emphasize socialization and environmental experiences – mainly events within the family – as being important in

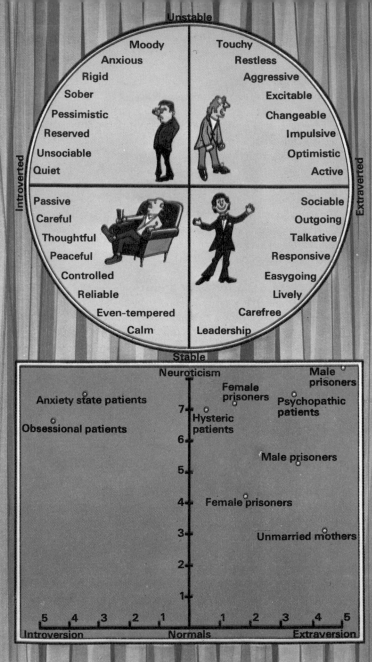

shaping the 'final' adult personality; those which stress the influence of heredity; and those which recognize that both heredity endowment and environmental experiences are important factors in determining the final personality.

Freud's theory of personality formation is an environmental one. In his view the adult's personality is a result of the way the young child copes with a series of crises within the family. Sometimes a child never does resolve a particular crisis and so he becomes fixated at a particular stage of development and the various types of neurotic personality disorders in adulthood arise as a direct result. Freud believed that all the main outlines of human personality are determined by experiences within the family before the age of four.

In Eysenck's view an individual's personality is determined by his hereditary endowment. An interesting experimental finding reported by Eysenck is that extraverts are harder to condition than introverts. This has led him to suggest that socialization comes about as a result of conditioning, and that a person's 'conscience' is simply a conditioned response which emerges as a result of the rewards and punishments administered by parents in their efforts to socialize the child.

The introvert conditions more easily than the extravert and so he is more easily socialized. Eysenck has reported findings which suggest that the criminal is typically an unstable extravert personality who, because he conditions poorly, is never adequately socialized, and therefore is more likely to retain behaviour not approved of by society. On this view the criminal's inability to be conditioned is inherited, because both the degree of extraversion and instability are genetically determined. These views seem to derive added weight from the recent findings in genetics which indicate that criminals possess a defective chromosome.

This idea is now particularly controversial because it runs counter to many currently accepted notions of the formation of the criminal personality, which tends to stress environmental causes.

(*Top*) Traits which characterize the four personality types. (After Eysenck) (*Bottom*) Results of introversion-extraversion and neuroticism tests in various groups.

Heredity and environment in personality formation

There are problems which arise in discussions of personality formation, genetics and environment. First, it cannot be said that personality types, for example criminals or schizophrenics, are genetically determined without any consideration of environmental factors. This is true generally, for instance it cannot be said that a man's height is genetically determined; it can only be stated that the difference between two mens' heights is genetically determined if and only if they are brought up in the same environment.

This is also true of heredity and personality: a claim that the criminal personality is inherited with no mention of environmental experiences is meaningless. All that can be said is that the differences in personality between two people are genetically determined only if they have exactly the same experiences.

Sheldon's body types. Ectomorph (*left*), mesomorph (*centre*) and endomorph (*right*).

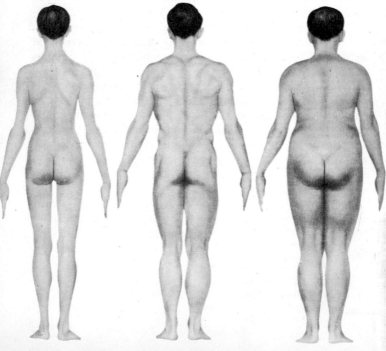

When it is argued that criminals are 'born', perhaps as a result of a possible chromosome defect, caution is required. It cannot mean that everyone born with such a genetic defect will become a criminal. It can only mean that they will have a greater disposition for criminal behaviour than other people, and probably, here, environment is crucial.

Body types and personality

The idea that the inheritance of a particular type of body build influences personality was suggested by Sheldon. He classified individuals according to three physical dimensions: endomorphic, mesomorphic and ectomorphic. The endomorphic component refers to a body build which has a predominance of horizontal over vertical build, and the endomorph is typically short and stocky. The mesomorph is athletic in build with wide shoulders and narrow hips. The ectomorph is usually tall, thin and stoop shouldered.

Parallel with these three different body types Sheldon identified three different personality types. The endomorph is supposed to be sociable and fond of physical comforts, the mesomorph was thought to be active, noisy and aggressive, and the ectomorph withdrawn and intellectual.

Personality tests

The psychologist has at his disposal test methods, which come from one of three different traditions, with which he can assess personality. These are the projective test, the objective test, and the attitude test traditions.

Projective tests are subjective measuring instruments. That is, a person's responses to a projective test are open-ended and capable of more than one interpretation by the tester. Two widely used projective tests are the thematic apperception test and the Rorschach test.

In the thematic apperception test the testee is presented with twenty ambiguous pictures; that is, each of these pictures is capable of many interpretations. The testee is invited to tell a story around each of them. 'Apperception' means a readiness on the part of the testee to interpret the pictures in certain ways which reflect conflicts and current anxieties. The tester (usually a psychiatrist or a clinical psychologist) looks for re-

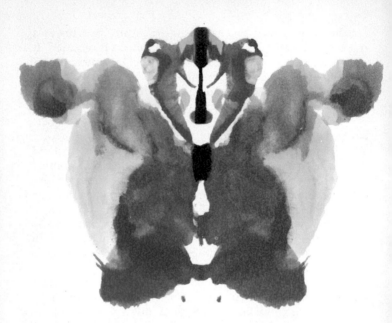

The Rorschach inkblot test.

current themes in these stories, and these are supposed to offer clues about these anxieties and conflicts.

The Rorschach inkblot test consists of a series of cards displaying an inkblot of various shapes and colours. The testee is required to tell the psychiatrist what he 'sees' in the card. This instrument relies on the tendency for most 'normal' people to see the same sorts of things in each of the inkblots. Any bizarre responses are interpreted by the psychologist as revealing unconscious aspects of personality.

Subjective tests are criticised by some psychologists because they rely too much on the interpretation of the tester, and because different testers make different interpretations of the same responses.

Objective instruments are usually paper and pencil tests which consist of a number of items or questions to which the testee is required to give one of the several answers supplied. The tests are objective because the responses are not open-ended, nor are they interpreted by the psychologist.

Attitude tests

One method of finding out about an individual's personality is to investigate his attitudes on a number of topics, for example, towards his friends, politics and himself. Many of the techniques used to treat mental illness are designed to change the attitudes of the patient. Usually a serious problem for him, when he undertakes a course of psychotherapy, is that he has an unhappy and possibly unrealistic set of attitudes particularly towards himself. The success of psychotherapy is determined partly by how these attitudes change, and if they do the patient can be regarded as having undergone, to some extent, a change in personality. It is important then to have available methods to measure these attitude changes.

One widely used instrument is the semantic differential which was developed by C. E. Osgood. This is used to find the meaning for an individual of various 'concepts' like mother, father, self, and so on. Osgood's investigations had previously shown that most normal people within a given culture tend to attach similar connotations and meanings to familiar concepts, and that psychiatric patients could be identified because their attitudes and meanings to these concepts deviated from the rest of the population.

In the thematic apperception test, subjects have to tell a story around a picture such as this.

A case of multiple personality

Cases of multiple personality in which an individual acts as if he is a completely different person on different occasions are rare. A famous instance of this was the case of the triple personality Eve White, and her associated personalities Eve Black and Jane.

Eve White was a serious-minded timid mother who had gone to the psychotherapist to have her severe headaches treated. During one of the sessions she had a sudden personality change to become instead an egocentric, wilful and promiscuous personality who called herself Eve Black. Eve Black and Eve White had been co-existing since early childhood, but Eve White had no idea of Black's existence until they had become acquainted with each other in the presence of the therapist. As the sessions proceeded a third personality, Jane, who was more mature than Eve White, appeared.

The distinctiveness of the various personalities was revealed when personality and handwriting tests by experts were given to the three. The semantic differential was also administered twice to Eve White, Eve Black and Jane, and this method too was able to discriminate between the three in terms of their attitudes towards various concepts like self, mother and father.

What conclusions can be drawn from this and similar cases? One is that those theories which attempt to correlate personality with a particular type of body build are patently wrong.

Another conclusion is associated with the basic assumptions of most personality theories. These assume that there is in each of us just one 'true' personality – an inner core that never changes. Eysenck's theory sets the view that a person categorized, for example, as a stable introvert, retains these personality characteristics whatever the situation and throughout his life.

Our own subjective experiences and those of Eve White suggest this view is not wholly true. We have in fact many selves, and we are all of us chameleon-like. So throughout every day we adopt, according to where we are and with whom, many different personalities and selves.

If this is true, then it would make the goals of most objective tests unrealistic. For they imply it is possible to trap a true and unchanging personality which is unaffected by different situations, people and mood. Moreover, they assume that attitudes once with us are incapable of change, and that as human beings we cannot learn.

The multiple personality of Eve.

MENTAL ILLNESS

Various forms of mental illness have been reported for almost every culture in the world. There are types of behaviour which could be considered perfectly normal in some societies, but grossly abnormal in others.

Thus it seems that what is called abnormal behaviour or madness is relative to a particular culture. In Britain to cry like a child and have hallucinations (experiences which occur in the absence of an appropriate external stimulus, for example, hearing voices or seeing objects) would be considered abnormal, yet this is perfectly normal for a Californian Indian in a religious trance.

If Britain is taken as a cultural setting, then among the mentally ill are those 116,000 men and women resident in mental hospitals. Leaving aside those mental illnesses which typically accompany old age, it is convenient to classify the remainder into two broad categories: the neuroses and the psychoses.

The neuroses
The neuroses consitute a cluster of symptoms which are the less severe of the two forms of mental disorder. The various

Admissions to US mental hospitals.

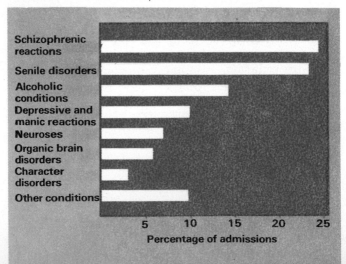

types of neuroses are classified according to their symptoms, but the one element they all have in common is anxiety. The symptoms of the various neurotic disorders have a function: to eliminate this anxiety.

A simple classification of the neuroses would include anxiety states, obsessional neuroses, hysteria and phobias. An anxiety state is one in which there is a very high level of experienced fear, and the symptoms show this; these patients typically suffer from a rapid pulse, dilated pupils and high blood pressure.

Hysterical neurotics frequently complain and have the symptoms of a physical illness. Practically any symptom of a physical disease may be imitated in hysteria, paralysis, vomiting, fits and headaches. Although hysterics actually do have these symptoms there appears to be no physical cause for them. Psychiatrists generally assume that these symptoms serve a function by being anxiety reducing. The anxiety of the patient is effectively eliminated by being converted into a physical symptom. Sometimes the symptoms of hysteria are mental and not physical and this can include amnesia, or in very rare cases, multiple personality.

Phobics are afflicted with irrational fears of certain kinds of

Number of patients in US mental hospitals. Improved techniques have caused a massive drop in cases.

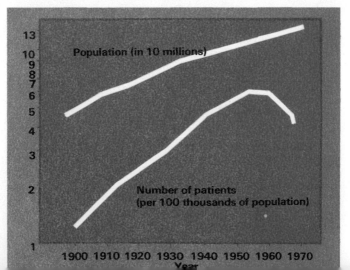

Population (in 10 millions)

Number of patients
(per 100 thousands of population)

1900 1910 1920 1930 1940 1950 1960 1970
Year

situations or objects in which there is no apparent danger. The phobic symptoms can be vague feelings of dread or fear, which are only relieved by avoiding the phobic situation. When a person does show phobic symptoms it is assumed by the psychiatrist or the psychotherapist that the place or object is associated with something that had been dangerous or threatening in the past.

Obsessional neurosis is most often characterized by an over-riding feeling of compulsion. The symptoms can be physical or mental, or both. The physical ones are marked by the tendency to repeat certain stereotyped or ritualistic acts. The mental symptoms are also compulsive in character, and include an overwhelming compulsion to think repeatedly about a particular subject, usually sexual.

Neurotic symptoms are defence mechanisms. Their function is to defend the individual against anxiety, and they are adopted unconsciously; that is to say, the person is unaware of either the anxiety or why he adopts his behaviour.

The psychoses
It is usual to categorize psychotic illnesses into either an organic psychosis or a functional psychosis. The organic psychoses constitute those mental disorders where a physical factor can be recognized as causing the disease; for example, damage to the brain tissues. A functional psychosis is one in which no apparent physical cause can be attributed to the disorder. In this account we will consider only the functional psychoses which include the two important classes of illness: the manic-depressive psychoses and the schizophrenias.

The manic-depressive psychotic is chiefly characterized by cyclical and exaggerated changes of mood, from 'normal' to either a manic-phase, marked by strong excitement and elation, to a depressed almost suicidal state. Each of the phases lasts over several weeks or even months.

Schizophrenia is the most common of all the psychotic disorders, and it accounts for about half of all the patients in mental hospitals. Contrary to popular belief, they are not the victims of a split or multiple personality – this is a confusion of schizophrenia with an extremely rare form of hysteria which constitutes one of the neurotic disorders.

Schizophrenic symptoms are many but they can, in general, be characterized by four traits. Firstly, schizophrenics typically do not exhibit emotion; they are dull and apathetic. Secondly, they lose interest in the people and events about them. They seem rather to react to the events of their inner life rather than those of the external world. Thirdly, schizophrenics are marked by the tendency to experience hallucinations and delusions (false beliefs). Fourthly, they are characterized by varying degrees of disturbance of thought; their speech is frequently incoherent and disconnected and, as the illness progresses, their intelligence and memory deteriorates.

Psychiatrists and clinical psychologists now classify schizophrenics into one of two categories: *process schizophrenics* and *reactive schizophrenics*.

The process patient usually has had a long history of

Researcher	Year	Percentage incidence of schizophrenia in both twins out of total no. of twins investigated	
		Non-identical	Identical
Rosanoff	1934	10·0	67·0
Slater	1951	14·0	76·0
Kallman	1952	14·5	85·6

Summary of studies of schizophrenia in non-identical and identical twins (*above*).
Relationship between class membership and incidence of schizophrenia in Great Britain (*below*).

Social class

deterioration in social adjustment which started in later adolescence or early adulthood. The chances of a complete recovery are not good. The reactive schizophrenic typically has had a fairly good record of pre-illness social adjustment, and the psychotic breakdown has usually been precipitated by an acute crisis. Unlike the process patient the reactive usually has a good chance of recovery.

There are three main types of explanation for the cause of schizophrenia according to whether they emphasize heredity, the environment or chemical factors in the brain.

A completely hereditary-based explanation would mean that any individual with the abnormal genes would become schizophrenic no matter what the environment. On the other hand, a wholly environmentalist explanation assumes that a particular set of external circumstances would produce schizophrenia in an individual no matter what his genetic make up.

As is usual, the widely accepted standpoint is a compromise. It recognizes that there are probably certain types of environment in which certain individuals who possess an inherited pre-disposition to schizophrenia will be at maximum risk, whereas individuals who live in the same environment, but do not possess the inherited pre-disposition, will not become schizophrenic.

There is good evidence for a genetic factor in schizophrenia. If a schizophrenic has an identical twin then, on average, in 46 of these cases out of 100 the other twin will also be schizophrenic. Moreover, the child of a schizophrenic parent has nearly a fifty per cent chance of being either a schizophrenic or to suffer from a related personality disorder. This finding does not remove the possibility of an environmental explanation, for the schizophrenic parent may transmit the illness to his children by a method of child-rearing rather than by genes.

Research on environmental factors and schizophrenia have concentrated on child care practices with a view to relating these to the incidence of schizophrenia. R. D. Laing, a British psychiatrist, argues that schizophrenia results from experiences within the family, and specifically to distorted communications and contradictory 'messages' between members of the family group.

Biochemical theories of schizophrenia suggest that the disorder is caused by an excess of some chemicals that are manufactured naturally in the brain.

The drugs LSD-25 and mescaline produce hallucinations and symptoms in normal people that resemble schizophrenic ones, and it has been shown that there are substances – serotonin being the most important – which occur in the body whose chemical structures are very similar to both LSD and mescaline.

The hypothesis is that schizophrenia is correlated with the presence of one of these LSD-type substances generated in excess in the brain, and cure can be brought about by the use of drugs which inhibit this excess production.

LSD is synthesized from the fungus ergot of cereals (*left*).
Psilocybin (similar in its effects to LSD and mescaline) is derived from the sacred mushroom (*right*).

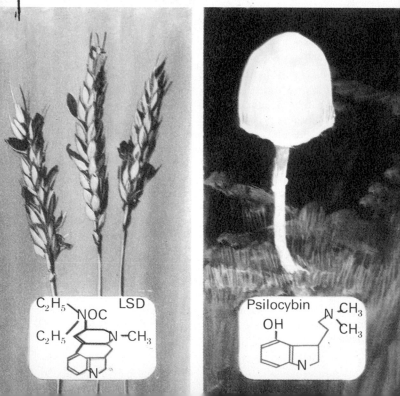

'Treating' mental illness by branding the head with hot irons.

The treatment of mental illness

The techniques used to treat the mental disorders can be approximately categorised into two kinds: physical methods and psychotherapy.

Physical techniques are used to change behaviour by physiological means, drugs, shock treatment or neurosurgery (removal of parts of the brain thought to be implicated in the mental disorder). Psychotherapy constitutes a class of treatments designed to bring about changes in behaviour through psychological methods, usually but not always by a process of communication between the patient and therapist. These techniques include psychoanalysis, behaviour therapy and group therapy.

The two treatment approaches reflect the rather different opinions as to the cause of mental disorders. The physical methods presuppose physiological, probably biochemical, explanations whereas the psychotherapeutic methods stress environmental causes and experiences in the life history of the patient.

Physical methods of treatment

One physical method widely used about twenty years ago, and less so now, is electro-convulsive therapy (ECT). This involved passing an electric shock through the brain to produce convulsive seizures and unconsciousness. It was particularly successful in curing severely depressed patients.

Drugs are now widely used in psychiatry for the control of symptoms. Two which are now extensively used, particularly for the treatment of psychotics, are chlorpromazine (largactil) and reserpine (serpasil). They not only calm the patient but they also significantly alleviate the hallucinations and reduce the extent of emotional withdrawal. So successful are these drugs, that in many cases of chronic schizophrenia patients have been first rendered amenable to psychotherapy and then eventually discharged from hospital.

Psychotherapy

Psychotherapeutic methods have been used more successfully with neurotic than with psychotic patients. For, unlike the

Rapid rotation was an eighteenth century 'cure' for mental illness.

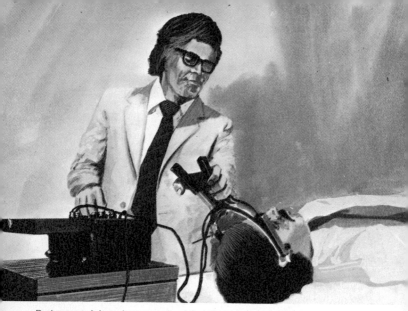

Patient receiving electro-convulsive therapy.

psychotic, the former are able to communicate with the therapist.

Psychoanalysis is used almost exclusively for the treatment of neurotic disturbances, and its method and theoretical basis derive largely from the work of Sigmund Freud. The psycho-analyst usually sees his patient for about an hour several times a week. The assumption behind the treatment is that a cure – a change in behaviour from neurotic to normal – is best achieved if the patient is made aware of his own unconscious motives and conflicts. To achieve this the patient enters into free association, that is, he is required to say anything that comes to mind and to withhold nothing from the psycho-analyst. This task, though difficult for a patient, eventually brings about an awareness of events, conflicts and wishes, usually in early childhood, which are currently a source of difficulty to the individual even though they may have long been forgotten and repressed.

Behaviour therapy refers to the treatment of mental illness by the use of principles derived from learning theory principally from the work of Pavlov and Skinner. Therapists using Skinner's methods have no special theory of neurotic behaviour, and their treatment uses operant conditioning techniques to control and modify neurotic symptoms.

Other behaviour therapists account for neurotic symptoms in terms of Pavlovian conditioning: the symptoms are viewed simply as maladaptive habits which reduce anxiety. In this country Eysenck has been closely associated with the Pavlovian concept of neurosis.

Eysenck sees himself as working from one of two assumptions in the treatment of neurotic disorders. One of these is that the patient has deficiencies in his learning, that is, he has not learned to produce normal adaptive good behaviour. A child who wets the bed is an example of this patient. The second assumption is that some patients have acquired conditioned responses which are in fact normal, and so the task of the behaviour therapist is to 'extinguish' these abnormal responses. (People with irrational fears or phobias are examples of these patients.)

Behaviour therapists regard the symptoms as the neurosis, whereas the psychoanalyst sees the symptoms as distress signals underlying those hidden conflicts which must be discovered before the patient can recover.

It has already been mentioned that behaviour therapists reject the disease concept of mental illness; for them the disorders are simply responses to external circumstances and do not issue from any psychic state within the individual. With respect to the fact that they reject the illness concept, they are in agreement with R. D. Laing (see page 80).

Group therapy is a form of psychotherapy which takes place when the same small group of patients (usually about six to twelve people), with the same sorts of problems, meet regularly together over a long period of time. The therapist or conductor remains in the background in order to allow group members to exchange experiences and discuss their own and other patients' symptoms.

At first the group members are defensive and uncomfortable about exposing their weaknesses, but they gradually become more objective about their own behaviour, and more aware of the affect their attitudes and behaviour have on others.

An important goal of group therapy is to socialize the patients. In a group therapy session they are allowed to work out their problems in the presence of others, observe how others react to their solution, and then try out alternative ways of behaving if the old ones fail. The aim is that the patient should carry these new ways of dealing with people to situations outside the therapy session.

Group therapy is used in a variety of situations including hospitals with both psychotics and neurotics, and with parents of disturbed children.

R. D. Laing and schizophrenia

An implicit assumption of traditional psychiatric thinking on mental illness has been that it is a disease process, either organic or psychological, which afflicts a person. The idea is that the mentally ill individual has undergone a process of pathological change, and is therefore required to submit to treatment in order to be cured.

This psychiatric model has now been sharply challenged by some psychiatrists – they call themselves 'anti-psychiatrists' – working mainly with schizophrenic patients, and the best known of these is R. D. Laing. His main conclusion is that schizophrenia is not a disease of one person, but rather a bizarre way in which whole families or even societies function.

Group therapy session.

Acute schizophrenia then is not an 'illness' but a social crisis situation in which one member of the group – usually a family – is elected by the other members to become the schizophrenic patient. One implication of this alternative view for the treatment of schizophrenia requires an understanding of the nature of this elective process.

For Laing, sanity and madness are social concepts, and normally a person is considered sane if his behaviour and utterances are intelligible to others. From this it follows that an individual previously classified insane can be restored to sanity by a psychiatrist who manages to achieve successful communication with him.

The task then for the psychiatrist treating schizophrenia, in the Laingian view, is similar to that of an anthropologist who seeks to understand the social system of an unknown tribe. For the world at large, its customs, language and behaviour appear strange and alien, but within the context of the tribe itself all these customs and goings-on have their own function and sense. So it is with the psychiatrist: his task is to chart a way and make sense of the private world of the psychotic. The behaviour of the schizophrenic is only apparently strange, for in reality his strange behaviour and utterances in fact compose a logical corpus of behaviour and language, in which perfectly natural demands are being made.

On this view insanity is a temporary failure to maintain socially acceptable channels of communication with other people. This breakdown in communication has its main cause and location in the family, and it is there that the members are recipients of wildly contradictory messages. The delusions of the schizophrenic are a withdrawal from direct or indirect communication with others, for an individual's image of himself and his attitudes are crucially determined by what he sees and understands as other people's conception of him. There is in each person a true self which must be accepted and confirmed by others, and if this validation is withheld by the family, or in childhood, the individual will lose confidence in his real identity and will resort instead to constructing a false self (which will be labelled schizophrenic behaviour). At the same time he will detach his true identity so that it will, so to speak, lurk in the shadows – never to be tested by confrontation with others.

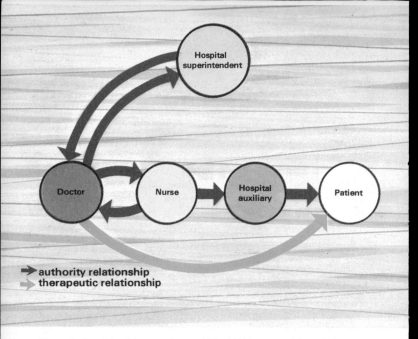

authority relationship
therapeutic relationship

Interrelationships in a pre-Second World War mental hospital.

The therapeutic community

It is not commonly realized that a profound revolution has occurred in British and American mental hospitals since the war, and the credit for the modern therapeutic community methods in these hospitals belong to psychiatrists practising group therapy with neurotic and psychotic inpatients.

In the mental hospitals of thirty years ago, the tasks, status and responsibility of each member of staff was sharply defined. The medical superintendent was at the apex of the hospital hierarchy. The psychiatrists managed the clinical problems and were answerable only to the superintendent. The senior nursing staff decided which patients constituted clinical problems and communicated this opinion to the doctor. The junior staff relayed their observations to the senior nursing staff but never to the doctors. The patients communicated with nobody – they were the recipients of the treatment.

Information and directives flowed entirely downwards and percolated to the patients via a number of well-defined layers,

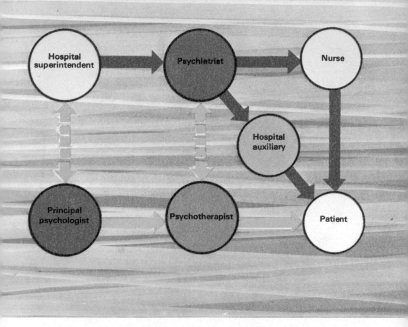

Interrelationships in a modern mental hospital.

and what information went up the hierarchy was modified and transformed in order to keep the authority structure intact, and to sustain a satisfactory if delayed image.

In a hospital whose wards are run on what are called therapeutic-community lines all the authority relationships are blurred. The professional staff and patient demarcation is minimized and so too is the senior and junior hierarchy. Doctors, patients, nurses, therapists, psychologists and ward orderlies all meet once a day for an hour or so to discuss what is happening and why.

So junior nurses criticize the psychiatrists, the patients question the cooks and the medical superintendent. Those who have experienced the introduction of the therapeutic-community methods report the bitterness and insecurity it brings, but they also report that if enough time is allowed to elapse – about a year – the group discussions become less destructive and critical and they become more centred on psychotherapy.

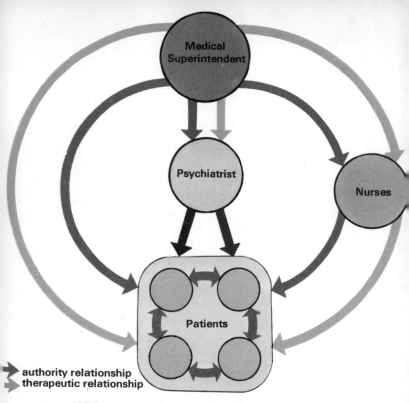

authority relationship
therapeutic relationship

Interrelationships in a hospital run as a therapeutic community.
Every relationship has both an authority and therapeutic aspect.

Is personality genetic, environmental or self determined?

The idea that our personality is a product of both our genetic endowment and environmental experience is now accepted by most psychologists. This is a deterministic viewpoint and it raises the question of whether individuals have any real choice in developing their own personality and controlling their own behaviour.

It is commonly supposed that a completely genetic explanation of human personality is more deterministic than an environmental one. There are a number of points to be made here. An hereditary determination of people's responsibility for their actions raises exactly the same questions of principle with respect to free will and responsibility as does any other form of determination.

It is probably felt that environmental explanations are less deterministic than genetic ones because it is easier to manipulate and control the environment than it is to control the genetic make up of individuals. Such a control is feasible, however, and the name *eugenics* is given to attempts to 'improve' a race by selective breeding according to genetic principles. It has been advocated by some in order to improve intelligence, physical strength, or perhaps some other personality attribute valued by a society.

Psychotherapy and social control

Through the use of drugs, along with behaviour therapy and the more traditional methods of psychotherapy, psychologists have devised many techniques for the control of behaviour. A patient's actions can be modified and 'improved' in order to make them more amenable to the accepted standards of conduct of a society. The way this is achieved differs according to the method used, but the result is the same.

An important question with respect to both eugenics and social control methods is: Who determines the values on which these supposed improvements are to be introduced?

It would have to be assumed that either some group of individuals within the society, or society at large, knows what the human race is here for, and knows what is best for the individual. In this context it can readily be seen that however benign the techniques used to alleviate mental illness, they can too easily become a method for social control by which to gentle the 'masses', and an instrument by which any recalcitrant individual or rebel, or perhaps that unconsenting self in us all, can be brought to heel and turned into a virtuous citizen of an always drab, always conforming, and very probably totalitarian society.

It is one of the strengths of R. D. Laing's views of mental illness and schizophrenia that he remains enormously sceptical about the sort of society the schizophrenic should be inducted back into, and his pessimistic vision questions very deeply the values of our own.

Sigmund Freud, the founder of psychoanalysis.

Carl Gustav Jung.

SLEEPING, DREAMING AND CONSCIOUSNESS

A recurring problem in modern psychology is that of consciousness. Each of us knows what it is like to remember, to be angry or to dream, but our thoughts, feelings and dreams are private and accessible to no-one but us. By conscious experience, we mean those events of which the person experiencing them is fully aware.

The early behaviourists in their revolt against a previous generation of psychologists and philosophers denied that consciousness could be studied. Their aim was to build a science of psychology in which the events to be observed were available to external objective observers. This revolt effectively precluded them from studying consciousness and so research into dreams, sleep and other states of consciousness ceased, and it has only recently been taken up again by experimental psychologists.

The behaviourists also sharply scrutinized the old philosophical problem of the relationship between the body and mind. They were particularly critical of the 'common sense view' that the body takes orders from the mind, and the body in turn limits to some extent the actions of the mind. This distinction is implicit in those views of mental illness which maintain that bodily illness can result from mental illness.

The behaviourists rejected the body–mind distinction and its two implied assumptions. The first of these was that it is the mind which gives rises to conscious experience, and the second was that the mind, and therefore conscious experience, functions on principles altogether different from the workings of the body.

The behaviourist revolution was in effect a denial of the proposition that there were two separate kinds of events in the world: mental events and physical events.

Freud, in his famous work, *The interpretation of dreams*, regarded dreams as the products of the conflict between the *conscious* controlling impulses of rational thought, and the primitive impulses from an individual's *unconscious* processes. By an unconscious process is meant those thoughts, wishes and fears of which the person is unaware, but which still influence his behaviour.

Freud believed that the socially unacceptable wishes of childhood are suppressed by the process of socialization, and they instead become part of an individual's active unconscious where they still remain influential.

The active unconscious finds its expression, according to Freud, in neurotic illness and dreams, as well as in socially accepted outlets like scientific and literary creativity. During sleep, primitive impulses and wishes come from the unconscious and rise towards conscious awareness. The conscious 'socialized' mind, however, censors them; it allows these impulses to enter, but clothes them in symbolism in order to make them more acceptable: the penis, for instance, becomes a cigar in the dream. In Freud's view all dreams are symbolic and have to be interpreted in order to find their underlying meaning.

Jung, a contemporary of Freud, had a more elevated idea of the nature of dreams. Where Freud had found in them only the sinister remnants of the unconscious, Jung saw dreams as expressions of religious and moral experience deriving from racially inherited ideas.

Recording brain activity during sleep on an electroencephalogram by attaching electrodes to the forehead and temples.

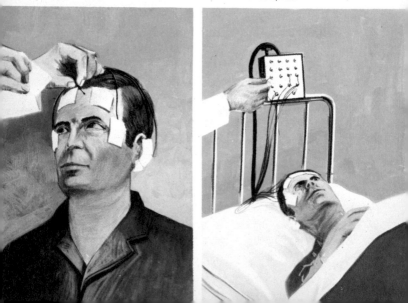

If a man reported a dream with an unknown woman in it, Freud assumed that the woman symbolized the man's mother. The dream was a reminder of his repressed desire for sexual relationships, and the woman remained unknown to the dreamer only in order to dupe the censorship imposed by the conscious mind. Jung, however, would have interpreted the unknown woman as an image – perhaps deriving from a collective unconscious – symbolizing the feminine aspects of a male dreamer's personality.

Modern research into the study of sleep

One tool used for research on sleep is the electroencephalogram (EEG). Using this it is possible to detect various stages of sleep by recording electrical discharges from the brain. The EEG can also be used for clinical investigation by physicians to detect neurological disorders. The patient who submits to an EEG examination has small metal discs sensitive to minute variations of electrical potential (electrodes) attached to the scalp. These variations are amplified and then fed to a writing device which records them on long rolls of paper. This record looks like a wave, and it is this which constitutes the electroencephalogram. EEG records show wave patterns occurring at different frequencies. If in a space of one second

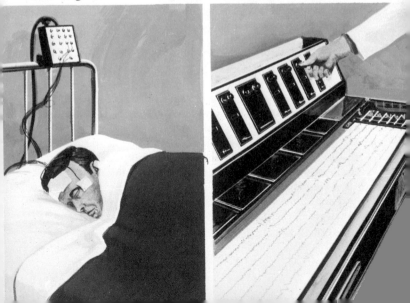

three waves occur, the frequency is said to be three cycles per second (cps). The electrical impulses also vary in size, that is to say they differ in amplitude. By examining both the frequency and amplitude of the EEG wave pattern, the research worker is able to do one of several things.

For instance, if a stimulus produces a change in the wave pattern recorded from one pair of the electrodes, but not in the patterns recorded from the rest, he infers that only the area to which the pair is attached is affected, and therefore there is probably damage in that particular part of the brain.

For normal individuals it is convenient to classify the wave patterns on the EEG records as being basically one of four types: *beta*, *alpha*, *theta* and *delta* waves.

Beta waves have frequencies of between 14 and 25 cps, alpha waves have frequencies of between 8 and 13 cps, theta waves are between 4 and 7 cps, and delta waves have frequencies between 3·5 and 0·5 cps. Generally speaking, delta waves are the largest waves and beta waves the smallest.

When the individual is relaxed but awake his EEG record shows alpha waves. When he falls asleep the record shows a change: the alpha waves disappear and they are replaced mainly by theta waves. This EEG pattern defines what is called stage 1 sleep. (Stage 1 occupies 20 per cent of night sleep.) As the individual continues to sleep another change appears: the waves become slower (lower frequency) and of higher amplitude than before. These EEG features characterize stage 2 sleep and if the individual is awakened he reports that he was sleeping lightly. (Stage 2 occupies 50 per cent of night sleep.)

Stages 3 and 4 can again be distinguished on the basis of the EEG records. Both stages show the appearance of delta waves of high amplitude and low frequency. In stage 3, delta waves occupy 20 to 50 per cent of the wave form while in stage 4 the delta waves occupy more than 50 per cent of the wave form.

Generally, in deep sleep the EEG wave forms are larger and of low frequency. In lighter sleep these waves become more rapid and more shallow, gradually shifting to the alpha frequency when the person is in the relaxed waking state.

(*Above*) Recording of the electrical activity of the brain. (*Below*) EEG recording of sleep stages. (After Dement and Kleitman)

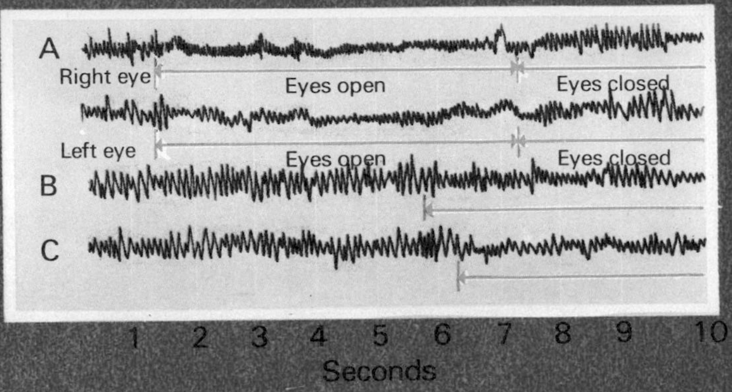

A

Right eye   Eyes open   Eyes closed

Left eye   Eyes open   Eyes closed

B

C

1   2   3   4   5   6   7   8   9   10

Seconds

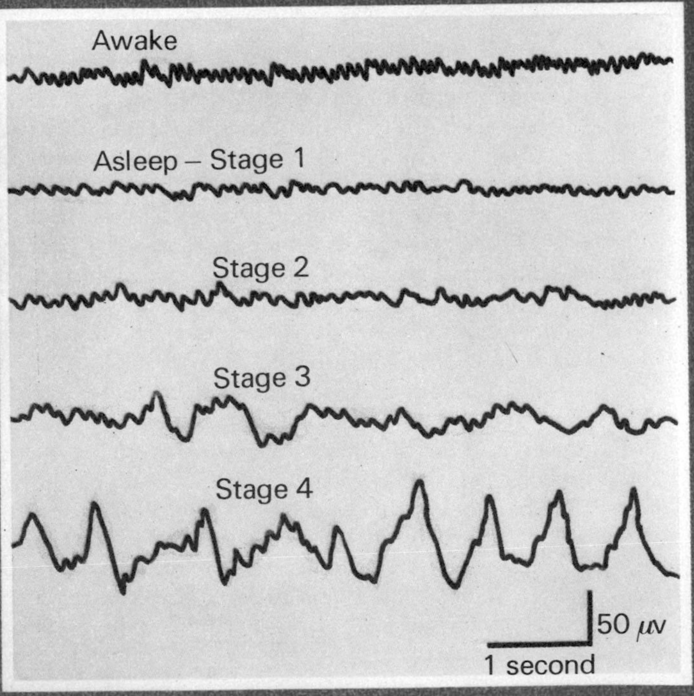

Awake

Asleep – Stage 1

Stage 2

Stage 3

Stage 4

50 μv
1 second

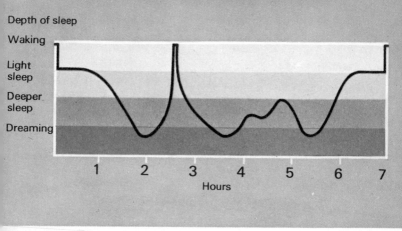

Depth of sleep

Waking

Light sleep

Deeper sleep

Dreaming

Hours

Alternation of sleep levels. (After Dement)

Eye movements and dreams during sleep

The apparatus used for recording and amplifying electrical discharges from the brain may also be used to record eye movements. For this purpose electrodes are attached at the sides of the person's eyes. The electrodes are sensitive to voltages that occur whenever the eyeballs move. When the resulting voltages are amplified and then recorded on a roll of paper by a movable pen the resulting record is called an electrooculogram, and the wave form which records eye movements looks very similar to the EEG.

In general it is easier to rouse someone from stages 1 and 2 than from 3 and 4. There is something peculiar about stage 1 sleep, however. It is only in this stage that dreaming occurs and it is very nearly always accompanied by rapid eye movements (REMS). During this period of stage 1 REM sleep it is very difficult to arouse the sleeper; if he is awakened, however, he always reports that he was dreaming. This dreaming state is often referred to as *paradoxical sleep*, because the sleeper on one criterion (EEG) is near to being awake, but hard to arouse by another (REMS).

How much time does a person spend in each of the sleep

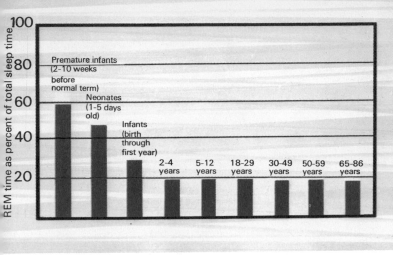

Decrease in REM time with increasing age. (After Kales)

stages? Obviously this varies from person to person, but for any one individual the sleep pattern is fairly consistent each night. On average a person spends about 20 per cent in stage 1, 50 per cent in stage 2 and 20 per cent in stages 3 and 4.

In the first hours of sleep very little dreaming occurs and it is usually made up of stages 3 and 4. Stage 1 REM sleep occurs in the last third of the night, and it is in this part of the night that dreaming occurs.

Why do rapid eye movements occur during dreaming?

This question is fraught with difficulties. A person in a sleep experiment may say he was dreaming simply to please the experimenter, and even if it is true that people report real dreams when awakened from REM sleep, why do REMS occur during dreaming? One theory is that the eye movements scan the visual image of the dream.

This immediately raises the question of whether blind people who presumably do not have visual dreams, have REMS during stage 1 sleep. Gross, Byrne and Fisher have reported findings on sleep research conducted on people who had been blind since birth, and their results seem to indicate that these people too have REMS during stage 1 sleep.

1. Baby sees ball placed under cloth on her left.

The experiment Piaget carried out on his daughter Jacqueline.

2. She retrieves it and the sequence is repeated.

3. Baby sees ball placed under cloth on her right but continues to search under cloth on her left.

INTELLIGENCE

Piaget and the mind of the child

How does the child acquire his knowledge of the world? Jean Piaget, until recently professor of psychology at the University of Geneva, has spent many years looking at just this question. Piaget has suggested that the intellectual development of human beings can be characterized by several stages through which it passes, and he has identified four great phases in the development of the human mind. These are the *sensori-motor* period, the period of *pre-operational thought*, the period of *concrete operations*, and finally the period of *formal operations*.

The sensori-motor period

The period of sensori-motor learning lasts from birth until about the age of two. In that time the child acquires an understanding of objects and actions and much of the behaviour of the infant appears to be instrumental learning – the learning of responses that are instrumental in obtaining a reward or a desired outcome. For instance, the child soon learns that if it cries it will obtain food and attention. Much of the child's activity in this period seems to be devoted to extracting correlations between actions and outcomes, as if deliberately varying his responses in order to test these outcomes. The impression is that the child is actively seeking knowledge of the external world.

During this time the infant also undergoes important changes in his understanding of the world. Particularly interesting is the way he seems to perceive objects. Even the simple idea that an object continues to exist regardless of the fact that he is not looking at it has to be learned; he acts as if an object is 'new' and different every time it reappears in his line of sight.

At first the child perceives objects not as independent entities, but as sensations inseparable from his attempts to see and hear. Later on, he begins to look for hidden objects – suggesting he has achieved some degree of separation of object from action – but he does appear to assume that the object of his search will always be found in its own special place, the place where it was first found.

Piaget has described how his daughter Jacqueline, at the age of ten months, watched her father place an object under a cloth on her left. She immediately retrieved it from the hiding place and the episode was repeated. On the third trial Jacqueline watched her father again place the object under the cloth but this time on the right of her. She continued to search for the object under the left cloth, however.

Why did she show this puzzling behaviour? Had she suffered from a lapse of memory? According to Piaget the child is *incapable* of remembering for she does not yet know she is dealing with a single object. For the child, the object under the left cloth is different from the object under the right: she has not yet attained the concept of *object permanence*.

The period of pre-operational thought

The period of pre-operational thought lasts from about the age of two to seven years. At this stage the child has now achieved the concept of object permanence, language development starts, and for the first time he begins to develop an internal representation of the external world.

The notion of an internal representation is a complex one. It certainly does not simply refer to the storage of facts in memory in the form of more or less faithful replicas of the original event. This is a fallacy perpetuated by such phrases as a 'photographic memory' which carry the implication that what is stored or represented in memory is a picture. An internal representation of the world must be one which exhibits abstract relationships between the facts of the world, and it is this which enables the child to exhibit truly intelligent behaviour. As he grows older so this representation becomes

more powerful and he is literally able to become more intelligent.

One interesting limitation of the thinking of the pre-operational child is that it is irreversible. He can imagine the outcome of a certain sequence of mental operations, but he is unable to return to the initial state. An example of this irreversibility in thinking is the water-glass problem. Suppose the pre-operational child is presented with two glasses, one tall and narrow and the other low and wide. When water is poured from the wide glass into the narrow one, it rises to a greater height than before. When the child is asked whether the new glass has the same amount of water in it as the old one he answers, 'no', whereas an older child will answer 'the same'. The pre-operational child has not yet acquired the concept of the conservation of quantity, and no amount of teaching will persuade him otherwise.

How can the difference between the less and more mature child be explained? How is the pre-conservationist view acquired and how is it replaced by a conservationist one? Psychologists have tended to put forward various 'appearance theories'; the child is carried away by appearances, or he is dominated by perception instead of logic. The usual psychological interpretation of the transition to a conservation view requires the development of some sort of reasoning capacity

If the contents of one of a pair of tumblers is poured into a shallow dish. the pre-operational child thinks the remaining tumbler holds more.

that allows the child to suppress appearances in favour of reasoning about the thing itself.

An alternative and more plausible view argues, on the contrary, that what we perceive depends on brain hypotheses and rules, and that the answer of the pre-operational child is perfectly logical. This view begins by not trying to explain the particular fact – the water-glass experiment – but to look for a more general rule or strategy the pre-operational child uses to compare quantities in everyday life. For instance, he divides a bottle of mineral water between two glasses by comparing levels. This strategy is usually sound because the glasses are the same size. This pre-conservation rule serves the child for most purposes even though he is sometimes wrong, especially when faced with a psychologist.

The period of concrete operations
The period of concrete operations lasts from about the age of seven to eleven and during this time logical deductions begin, although the child is still limited to reasoning about concrete operations. He has now achieved the concept of conservation of quantity and he is beginning to develop the idea of compensation: that one dimension (height) can compensate for another (width).

The development of intelligence through the period of concrete operations can be traced by presenting a child with two balls of plasticine of the same size and weight. If one of them is then shaped like a sausage, the pre-operational child will say that quantity, weight and volume have all changed. The child in the early stages of concrete operations now appreciates that quantity is unchanged, but still believes that both the weight and volume of the plasticine is altered. Later he realizes that both quantity and weight are unchanged, but persists in the belief that volume has altered. It is not until he is about eleven that the child realizes that volume, too, is unaltered.

The period of formal operations
The period of formal operations starts round about the age of eleven and lasts through adolescence until at last the final shape of adult intelligence emerges. He develops the ability to

engage in truly abstract reasoning, and his thinking is really unfettered from dependence on the environment. His internal representation of the world is now sufficiently powerful to make it unnecessary to actually execute an action in order to determine its consequences. Instead the entire sequence of events can now be anticipated internally.

If one of two balls of plasticene (1) is rolled into a sausage, the pre-operational child imagines both the weight (2) and volume (3) have increased.

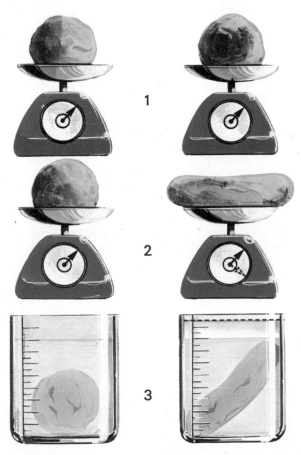

Approaches to the study of intelligence

In psychology there are now a number of standpoints from which to investigate intelligence. One of these is intelligence testing, the obtaining of a score which gives an individual's intelligence quotient (IQ). This approach evades the whole issue of the nature of intelligence; instead it concentrates upon differences in the ability of individuals to solve tasks which by general agreement are thought to require intelligence.

Another standpoint is that of Piaget and his colleagues. These workers ignore the individual differences that exist among individuals as measured by IQ scores, and instead they concentrate on identifying stages in the development of the intelligence of the human being.

Another approach stems from the theoretical advances made in computer science. The general name for this community of ideas which derive from these advances is artificial intelligence, usually abbreviated to AI. The central concern of AI is to program computers to do intelligent things: play chess, understand language, recognize objects, remember and solve problems. AI is not at all concerned with whether human beings think or behave by using the same processes as a computer, it is more concerned with arriving at an abstract theory of intelligence.

The general approach to writing programs that can solve intellectual problems is illustrated by considering the game of draughts. This game exemplifies the fact that many problems can in principle be solved by trying out all possibilities – in draughts by exploring all possible moves that an opponent might make in response to the other player. Programs for accomplishing 'intellectual tasks' have used this trial and error technique, and have capitalized on the computer's enormous speed to work out and 'search' all the possible combinations.

Programs have also had incorporated in them a collection of rules of 'where to search' and 'when to stop', thus cutting down the number of possible moves to be considered. What was significant about such programs was not the trial and error methods they used, but the embodied techniques that allowed the program to 'size up' the situation and choose a response. These programs only 'search' and 'look ahead' the first few alternatives, and then decide the response. A program that makes such judgements about what is best to try next is termed *heuristic* and it is this component which makes for intelligent behaviour.

Intelligence tests are psychological measuring instruments designed to measure individual differences in intelligence. The testee is required to solve a series of problems of varying difficulty, and the number of correct solutions gives a quantitative idea of his intellectual performance by comparing his score with that of other individuals of the same age.

The IQ of the testee indicates his position in relation to the population as a whole, and as such the IQ is a measurement of the intellectual development of a testee in relation to the average value for persons of the same age.

For a particular age group the average IQ is always put at 100, and 70 per cent of the individuals have an IQ in the range of 85 to 115, and 5 per cent have IQ's either below 70 or above 130.

Normal distribution of IQ for a population whose average is 100 IQ points.

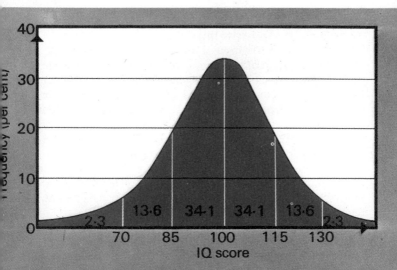

Are the observed differences in performance in intelligence tests due to heredity or to environmental experiences? A strictly environmentalist view is that if all individuals were to be given exactly the same experiences, there would be no differences in IQ scores between them. A strict heredity standpoint argues that early chilhood experiences, culture, and life-style – in short environmental circumstances – have no effect on the IQ scores, and the differences are due solely to differences in genetic endowment between people.

Nowadays, the 'either environment or heredity' approach to the problem is seldom made to account for IQ differences. Instead it is generally accepted that IQ differences between individuals are due to contributions from both environmental experiences and genetic endowment, and the question has rather become: What proportion do these two sources contribute to the differences in IQ found between individuals?

Heredity refers to those characteristics of an individual that are inherited from past generations. The gene is the essential element in the transmission of hereditary characteristics. Traits such as intelligence and personality characteristics are very probably influenced by the combined action of many genes.

Hebb's theory of intelligence

Piaget's theory of intellectual development does not seek to give an explanation of *why* people differ in intellectual ability. Donald Hebb of McGill University, however, has attempted not only to give a theory of the child's intellectual development, but also an explanation as to why people do differ in intelligence.

Hebb has suggested that intelligence has two components which he calls A and B. Intelligence A is innate and is determined by the quality of a child's brain structure at birth. Good initial brain structures can potentially develop better capabilities than poorer ones. The differences in component A found among individuals are genetic in origin.

To account for intellectual development, Hebb assumed that at birth the mind of a child is a blank, and the brain is simply a mass of neurones and tissue which have no specific functions for perceiving, remembering or language. As the child interacts with the environment so the brain develops structures to enable it to remember, to recognize, to use language and to think; that is to engage in intelligent activity. Because there are variations due to heredity in the quality of the child's brain structures, the same experiences with an

Jean Piaget

identical environment will have different effects on different people.

Hebb's intelligence B refers to the present functioning of the brain and is the component measured by IQ tests. Performance, on an intelligence test, therefore, is a combined measure of intelligence A (which is subject to genetic variation), and a contribution which is derived from early experience, environmental and other cultural effects which help build up the brain structures.

Twin studies and intelligence

The occurrence of identical and non-identical twins offers methods of separating out the relative proportions of environmental and heredity contributions to the observed differences in test scores between people.

Identical twins come from the same egg and are thus genetically identical. Any differences in IQ observed between them must be due to environmental experiences. Non-identical twins are as genetically similar as ordinary siblings

IQ differences between members of identical twin-pairs are usually low. (After Newman)

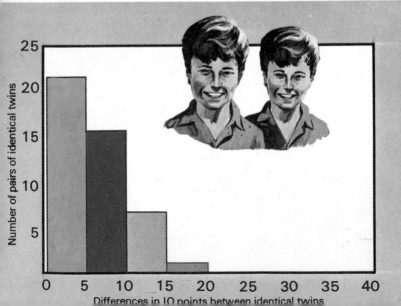

Number of pairs of identical twins

Differences in IQ points between identical twins

By comparing the degree to which identical and non-identical twins differ, and by making certain assumptions about environmental influences, it is possible to assess the relative contribution of genetic factors in determining IQ differences.

In one study, identical twins were found to have an average IQ difference of 5·9 points, whereas the average IQ difference for non-identical twins was 9·9. From this, it has been argued that because both sorts of twin member live in the same environment, then the observed IQ differences must be almost completely genetic in origin. This conclusion, however, does not take into account that the rearing conditions of identical twin pairs are probably more similar than for non-identical pairs. Identical twins are treated alike, clothed alike and they are necessarily of the same sex. On the other hand, non-identical twins, who are not as similar in appearance, are often treated quite separately, especially if they are of the opposite sex.

To avoid this difficulty, sets of identical twins which had been separated at or soon after birth were investigated, and

IQ differences between members of non-identical twin-pairs are usually larger than for identical twin-pairs. (After Newman)

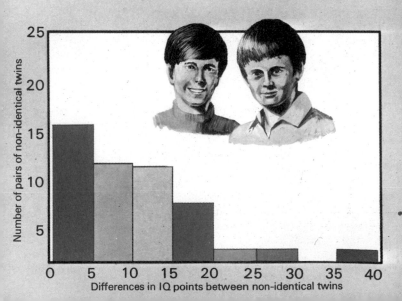

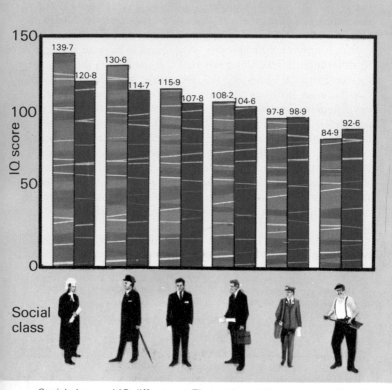

Social class and IQ differences. The red bars indicate average IQs of children from these classes. (After Burt)

the average IQ difference between them was found to be 8·8 points. This result for identical twins reared apart leads to the conclusion that different environments do not affect their IQ scores very much, and the major factor in determining intelligence test performance is therefore genetic. But how different were the rearing conditions for the twins reared apart? They were probably not very different. Whether separation of twins is arranged by adoption societies or by the parents the chances are that both will be placed in very similar types of home.

Social class and intelligence

Sir Cyril Burt has reported, as have other psychologists before him, that there are significant differences in average IQ among the children and parents from different socio-economic groups in Britain. Socio-economic level was classified on the basis of type of occupation into six classes. Class one included university teachers and others of similar standing in the professions, while class six included unskilled and manual workers. The main finding of Burt's study was that people from social class one possessed the highest average IQ, and those from class six the lowest. Moreover, the difference in average IQ between the highest and lowest socio-economic groups is over fifty points.

These findings are often used to support the view that the differences in average IQ between the various socio-economic groups are due mainly to genetic causes. Parents with low IQ tend to produce children with low IQ. As such, however, this is no evidence against environmental factors: intelligent parents naturally provide a highly stimulating environment for their children, and so might well give rise to a greater ability among them even though heredity played no part.

The opinion that these IQ differences favour an heredity explanation must be tempered with a certain amount of caution about what the tests do in fact measure. Attitudes, aptitude, personality and ability are all abstract notions and are also to a great extent undefined, and so it is difficult to know which of the psychological attributes is being measured.

Intelligence tests, for instance, do in part probably measure what is intuitively called intelligence, but very few psychological measuring instruments are 'pure'. That is to say, these tests simultaneously measure many other ingredients apart from intelligence, such as attitudes and social class membership. To overcome the problem of 'purity', intelligence tests and other psychological measuring instruments should only be used on homogeneous populations. An homogeneous population consists of a collection of individuals who are similar in many different ways, for instance, in type of education, upbringing, social class membership and attitudes.

If the same intelligence test is used on all social groups, then to compare the IQ scores of people from the different social classes reveals little. The test may well pick up the intelligence of an individual from each of these different social classes, but it will also pick up other ingredients specific to each of the social groups and this will contribute to the observed IQ score.

The problem of what psychological tests do in fact measure is largely unsolved, and it is concerned with what is called *test validation*. An IQ test is valid if it can be established that it measures intelligence and nothing else. Since this is impossible to achieve in practice, intelligence tests must be 'validated' for a particular homogeneous group.

To escape from the difficulty of the inapplicability of using intelligence tests on groups which are not homogeneous (such as using the same test on individuals from the different socio-economic groups, or comparing the average IQ of populations from different cultures such as American blacks and whites), attempts have been made to devise culture-free tests. Culture-free tests are supposed to be uninfluenced by a particular environment or culture.

It is said that those intelligence tests which measure linguistic skills, verbal reasoning and school subjects are more prone to environmental influences than culture-free tests.

There is no clear-cut evidence whether these two types of intelligence tests are more or less susceptible to environmental influences. It is more likely the case that each is sensitive to different kinds of environmental influence.

Race and intelligence

A. R. Jensen, a Harvard educational psychologist, has drawn attention to IQ differences between American blacks and whites. Jensen reported that the average difference in IQ scores between blacks and whites lies between 10 and 20 IQ points. Further, 95·5 per cent of the blacks have an IQ below the white average of 101·8, and 18·4 per cent have an IQ of less than 20, whereas only 2 per cent of the whites fall within this range.

To account for this racial difference in IQ, Jensen has urged that the major cause is genetic and the environmental differences between the two races have little effect. A finding that Jensen cites is that the blacks score worse on culture-free tests than on those tests which are alleged to be more sensitive to cultural influences. The conclusion was that environmental effects must play very little part in determining the average IQ differences between the two races. Such a conclusion, however, depends crucially on whether there are, in fact, culture-free tests.

The arguments presented by Jensen are complex and sophisticated and the only empirical way to disprove Jensen's contention unequivocally would be to compare a sample of black and white children brought up in strictly comparable environments.

On balance, most studies do show an average IQ for Ameri-

IQ differences between American blacks and whites. (After Kennedy)

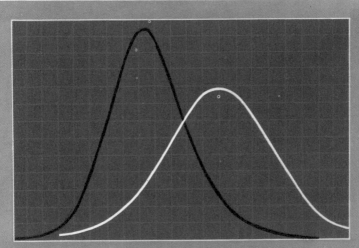

80·7   100·0

IQ score

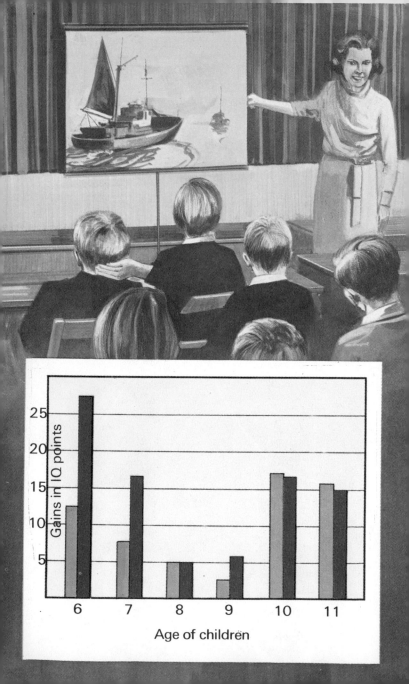

Gains in IQ points

Age of children

can black children which is lower than that for white children. What has not been shown is that these differences cannot be accounted for by the environmental differences between the two races, by the nature of the intelligence tests.

Much has been said about environmental effects on intelligence test performance, and Hebb's notion of intelligence B suggests that they are an important contribution to the observed IQ differences between people.

One environmental factor which it has been suggested might account for social class differences in average IQ is language. Basil Bernstein has proposed that different ways of communicating (codes) exist for each of the working and middle classes in Britain. These codes are supposed to reflect the different ways of thinking which are held to be directly responsible for the observed IQ differences between these two social classes.

Teacher expectation and intellectual performance

Another important environmental influence largely ignored by Jensen is the effect of the teacher and society expectations on children's intellectual performance. If for example children are expected to do badly at their school work, and this expectation is communicated by 'streaming' pupils – putting them for instance in classes according to ability – how does this expectation of future progress influence a child's actual performance? Or, if it is somehow communicated to individuals that they are discipline problems, how does this preconception by others affect their behaviour? This concerns the general problem of the self-fulfilling prophecy, and it concerns those predictions of future events that become important factors in bringing about that predicted event.

Two American investigators, Robert Rosenthal and Lenore Jacobson, studied just this question and they were interested, in particular, in the effect of teacher's prophecies or expectations of their pupils intellectual performance, and how it actually determines that intellectual performance.

Right-hand bars of each age group indicate IQ gains of 'expected spurters'; left-hand bars, of other children.

These two workers persuaded a school to cooperate with their investigation by pretending they were conducting a scientific study on the performance of certain pupils in the school who, they said, were about to make an intellectual spurt. The teachers were handed a test and asked to administer it to all their pupils. The teachers were led to believe that the test was specially designed to detect pupils who were going to make a spurt within the next few months.

After Rosenthal and Jacobson had scored the test, they selected a number of pupils at random and gave their names to the teachers who were told that these were the pupils who were going to make a spurt. The experimenters were primarily interested in the subsequent intellectual progress of these children compared with the rest of the children. The test was not in fact one designed to detect spurters. It was an ordinary though unfamiliar intelligence test.

The results were clear: compared with all other pupils the 'spurters' showed significant increases in IQ scores. Their behaviour and classroom conduct improved, and it was concluded that the teacher's favourable expectations can be responsible for gains in their pupil's IQs.

Caution is required when interpreting these seemingly gratifying results. The teachers reported that they did not remember the original list of 'spurters', and that the tests used to measure the IQ gains were not designed for the age group of the youngest children, yet it was for these for whom the greatest gains in IQ were recorded. The Rosenthal and Jacobson study did not reveal anything not known before; most teachers already know that their expectations have a powerful effect on their pupils progress and behaviour. What is not known, and what this study did not provide, was any understanding of the process by which teacher's expectations are communicated to the pupil.

The implications of this study are nevertheless disturbing. Can the failure of pupils in underprivileged areas be attributed to the negative expectations of society and teachers for these children? Do discipline problems and delinquency arise because teachers expect them to? Does streaming in schools perpetuate a self-fulfilling prophecy?

Example of an intelligence test

(1) Fill in the missing numbers
   (a) 1, 2, 3, 6, 12, __, __
   (b) 16, 2, 14, 3, 11, 4, __, __
   (c) 2, 3, 10, 12, __, __, 21, 22

(2) Cat is to dog as oak is to
   (a) tree
   (b) forest
   (c) beech
   (d) branch

(3) The following message is coded as shown
   THE TRAINS ARE LATE
   174 189523 984 6914
   —decode the following message.
   8913*5 + 4 92·*42

(4) Macbeth is to Hamlet as King John is to
   (a) The Merchant of Venice
   (b) Henry VI
   (c) The Taming of the Shrew
   (d) King Lear

Both marbles are moving round the same circle. The circumference of the circle is 20 feet. The red marble is moving at 5 feet a second and the blue marble is moving at 10 feet a second.

The red and brown marbles are moving in the same straight line. The distance between the two marbles is 10 feet. The red marble is moving at 16 feet a second and the brown marble at 21 feet a second.

(5) Does the blue marble or the brown marble hit the red marble first?

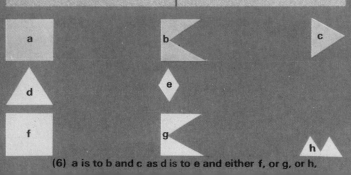

(6) a is to b and c as d is to e and either f, or g, or h,

There are other implications in this study and they concern the research methods. These involved underhand methods to obtain the teachers' cooperation, and both they and the children were treated simply as objects in an experiment. The reply of those psychologists who enlist such cooperation in bad faith is that there are no other ways to obtain the knowledge required.

One of the lessons to be drawn from this study seems to be that there are attitudes prevalent in schools to which children should not be exposed: among those is the attitude that knowledge is so important that it does not matter how it is acquired.

Environmental influences on brain development

Hebb's theory emphasizes the importance of early environmental experience on the development of intelligence. Some – which he termed 'enriched' – environments provide a good opportunity for the development of brain structures necessary for intellectual growth, while other more impoverished ones inhibit the development of such structures.

Rats in impoverished (*below*) and enriched (*opposite*) environments.

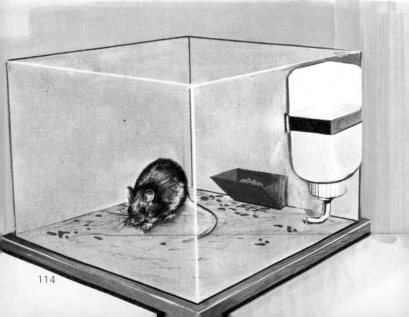

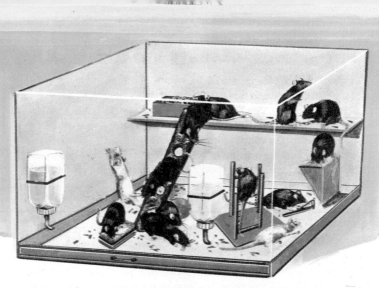

It is not known for certain what constitutes either a normal, or stimulating, or impoverished environment. There are many experiments, however, in which animals have been raised under stimulating or deprived conditions. Krech, Rosenzweig, Bennett and Diamond compared two sets of rearing conditions using rats. Some of them were reared in groups with runways, swings and other play equipment, and this formed the enriched or stimulating environment. The 'deprived' animals were reared alone in small bare cages with little opportunity to explore. The 'enriched' rats performed better on learning tasks later on in life, and they also showed measurable changes in brain tissue when compared with the deprived rats.

For human beings it is now generally believed that early childhood experiences, stimulation, or lack of it, have important consequences on later emotional and intellectual development. It may then be, that in the lower socio-economic groups, or in the typical black home in America, that some factors necessary for this stimulation are missing.

Yet it becomes all to easy to slide from such imprecise terms as 'impoverished environments', 'deprivation', 'underprivileged homes', and the like, into more condemnatory categories which serve only to justify a preconceived way of life, while at the same time expressing implicit disapproval or puzzlement at other ways.

INTELLIGENCE, MINDS AND MACHINES

There are two widespread ideas about men and computers. First, that machines can be built that do most of the things men can do – solve problems, 'remember' and read cheques. Second, that men are not only like machines, but *are* machines.

These ideas are not new. In the seventeenth century Descartes argued that animals were simply machines while man was part machine – the body – and partly mind. He likened the heart to a hydraulic pump, the veins to tubes, and animal brains worked by means of pieces of clockwork. All these analogies were derived from the machines of the day.

Animals were thought to be devoid of consciousness: they could not think, and the cry of a cat dissected by Descartes was construed as the noise of breaking machinery. Although the human body was a natural object and worked on the same principles as objects from the rest of nature – that is it obeyed the laws of physics and chemistry – the same principles could not be invoked to explain the mind of man. Mind, on Descartes scheme, was discontinuous with the rest of nature, but it was this which raised him above the animals and gave him his unique capacity of consciousness, language and thought.

Computers, brains and information
Nowadays attempts to understand the mind *are* made in terms of analogies with machines. The most complicated machine today is the computer. On this view, the brain is

regarded as a complex machine which processes information (stimuli) from the environment.

The incoming information, referred to as input, can be stored, and retrieved by the 'brain-computer'. Whatever operations are performed on the input, the brain initiates a response, a solution to a problem or an answer to a question. In computer jargon the response is referred to as the output.

A computer, whether it is storing data or performing complex operations on the input is, like the brain, essentially a device for dealing with information. The physical structure of a computer – the transistors, magnetic storage tapes and so on – is referred to as computer hardware. In the same way 'brain hardware' includes neurones and other brain tissue.

Computer software and brain software

A program is a recipe, a list of commands which instructs the computer exactly which operations are to be performed on the input. Computer programs form part of what is now called computer software.

When a programmer is presented with a specific problem for a computer, the first step is usually to draw a flow diagram.

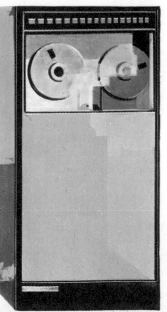

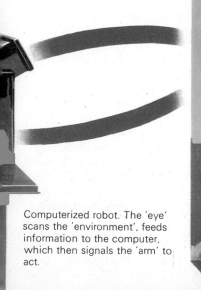

Computerized robot. The 'eye' scans the 'environment', feeds information to the computer, which then signals the 'arm' to act.

This is a pictorial analysis of the problem broken down into smaller logical units. From here, the problem is translated into a programming language, and the result is a computer program.

Some psychologists, who call themselves cognitive or experimental psychologists, see their task as understanding how the brain deals with input information or environmental stimuli when it is engaged in remembering, solving problems, or some other mental activity. For them this amounts to discovering the brain-computer programs which are in operation for each of these different activities. In the psychological laboratory the experimenter is usually aware of the inputs and outputs to a subject's brain, and the aim is to discover the particular program which operates on a given input to produce the observed output.

Just as a knowledge of computer hardware will not identify the program being used, so a knowledge of neurophysiology or brain hardware will be of no use to a psychologist who wants to find out what goes on in mental processes.

Computer simulation

An increasingly common way to express explanations about mental processes is the technique of computer simulation. A computer simulation of a psychological process consists of writing a program which attempts to mimic or imitate some aspect of behaviour whose explanation is required.

Newell, Simon and Shaw used this technique to account for the mental processes going on during problem solving by human subjects. They wrote their program to solve these problems by first observing how the subjects tackled them. The program was then run on a computer, and its performance and method of solution was compared with that of the subjects. Any discrepancies between the two were resolved by altering the program in such a way that the performance of the computer and that of the subjects was identical. When this was finally achieved Newell, Simon and Shaw claimed they understood the mental activity underlying human problem solving, and that the computer program itself constituted a

Flow diagrams to find the average of two numbers (*left*) and 100 numbers (*right*).

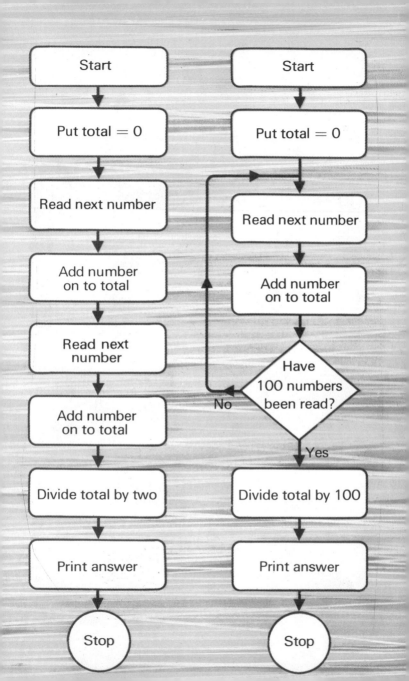

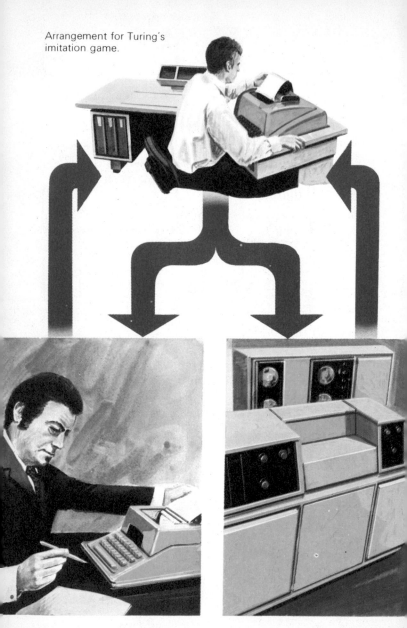

Arrangement for Turing's imitation game.

theory of this mental activity.

Work of this kind inevitably raises the question: Can machines think? Alan Turing, an English mathematician, considered this same problem and he rephrased it: Is it possible for a computer to behave in the way we behave when we say we are thinking? To answer this he proposed his imitation game.

Turing's imitation game

In the imitation game a computer is compared with a human subject in terms of the answers it gives to a questioner. The questioner, who is not allowed to see either the computer or the subject, sends a question to them both on a teletyper. The replies to the question return, also via a teletyper, so the interrogator has no visible means of discovering whether the subject of the computer is answering the question. Both man and computer reply to each enquiry. The aim of the interrogator is to frame questions in such a way that the identity of the respondent is revealed. If the questioner is unable to decide whether the machine or subject answered the enquiry then Turing suggested that the computer must be behaving in a 'human' manner.

In the Newell, Simon and Shaw experiment both machine and subject would be asked to solve questions in logic. The machine had been programmed, however, to make even the same kinds of mistakes as the subject, and so it would be impossible on Turing's criterion to decide which of the two had answered the question.

This general approach, to what is now called *artificial intelligence* studies, is contributing to a deeper understanding of intelligence and thinking. To many, such an approach seems to betray a philosophy and an image of man which is both ugly and inhuman. For those who think this way there is perhaps a confusion of the belief that human beings ought not to be treated as if they were natural objects with the belief that they are not in reality natural objects.

To say that we are natural objects, continuous with the rest of nature, is in no way a licence to manipulate and control other people in the way we as scientists seek to manipulate and control other objects found in nature.

LANGUAGE

Within the last ten years psychologists have concentrated much research and effort into the study of language, and this new area of investigation has become known as *psycholinguistics*. There are a number of problems in which the psycholinguist is interested. How do children learn language? What is the relationship between language and thought? Does language determine the way we think? Is language a uniquely human ability, and should we therefore expect to find evidence of any language ability in animals? Would it be possible to build computers that understand a natural language like English or French?

To understand recent developments in psycholinguistics it is necessary to consider briefly language structure. Structure refers to those features or components which are present in all languages. Another expression, often used for such features, is language universals. One example of a language universal is the sentence itself. A sentence, however, is not simply a group of words strung haphazardly together: every language possesses a grammar or syntax which specifies the rules by

René Descartes, founder of modern philosophy.

which words are combined to form meaningful sentences.

Another universal component to be found in all languages is the word. Words can usually be broken down into simpler units of meaning. These basic units of meaning are called *morphemes*. Consider the word badness. This word consists of two units of meaning or two morphemes: bad and ness (ness implies having the quality of). Some words, it will be noticed, are themselves morphemes: strange and ceiling are both single morphemes since these words cannot be subdivided into smaller units of meaning.

Yet another universal component is those relatively few basic sounds of a language which when combined in various ways form a word. It is an interesting fact that while the vocal apparatus of man is capable of producing an incredible variety of different sounds, each language consists of sounds which are a combination of a very few basic sounds or *phonemes*. English has about forty-five phonemes, some languages have as few as fifteen, while others have as many as eighty-five. This means that any word in English is made up of some combination of phonemes from among the forty-five possible.

Whorf's hypothesis

What is the relationship between the language we use and our way of thinking? It is commonly assumed that reality exists independently of the way we talk about it, and that any *idea* expressed in one language can be translated into another. Whorf, however, an American anthropologist who studied Red Indian languages, found direct translation of ideas from some Indian languages to English impossible, and he came to two rather surprising conclusions. These were, firstly, that the world is conceived differently by those whose language is completely different; and secondly, that it is the language itself which is the cause of these different ways of conceiving the world.

Whorf's suggestion has become known as the *linguistic relativity hypothesis* because it proposes that thought and ways of thinking are relative to the language in which it is conducted. So on this view, members from different cultures and having different languages differ in the way they think of and conceive the world.

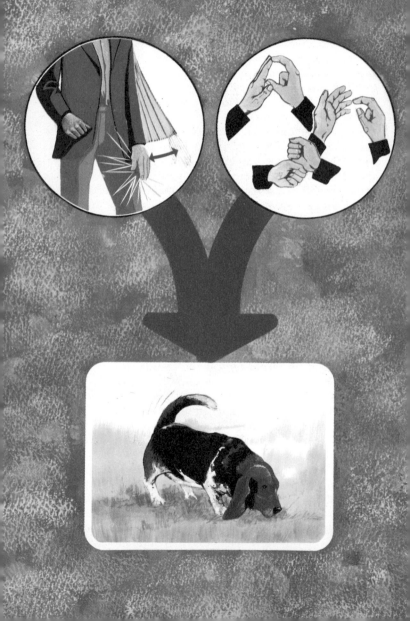

The word 'dog' conveyed by a single ASL gesture (*left*) and by two-handed deaf and dumb gestures (*right*).

One interesting variant of Whorf's hypothesis has been used by Basil Bernstein. Instead of investigating people from different cultures and with different languages, and examining the ways in which their thinking differs, he has instead looked at two groups of people who share the same language (English) and come from the same culture (Britain), but who come from different social classes. Bernstein's aim was to compare their different modes of thinking, and to try to relate it to the different ways each of the social classes use the same language. Bernstein was originally concerned with trying to explain the differences in IQ between the lower and higher socio-economic groups, and he suggested that people from these different social classes in fact speak different languages: *elaborated codes* and *restricted codes*.

The elaborated codes are used by the middle classes and the restricted codes by the working classes. Although the vocabulary in both these codes is the same, Bernstein claims that the two codes constitute different ways of using the same vocabulary and it is this which gives rise to two very different modes of thinking. It is then further argued that current IQ tests are more sensitive to the thinking produced by elaborated code users, than to the modes of thought produced by restricted code users. From there, Bernstein argues that IQ tests favour and have an inbuilt bias for elaborated code users or middle-class children.

The language of the deaf and dumb
The general problem of the connection between language and thought is highlighted in studies which have compared the intellectual competence of deaf and dumb subjects with normal subjects of the same age. Some psychologists have argued that because in their opinion language is essential for thought, then deaf children would be unable to do as well in intellectual tasks as normal children of the same age. Many of the comparisons that have been made are not clear cut, but on balance it does seem that deaf children are behind normal children in intellectual development.

Caution is required, however; this intellectual lag cannot be attributed to the lack of language in the deaf children. It is tempting to assume that it is the ability to use the organs of

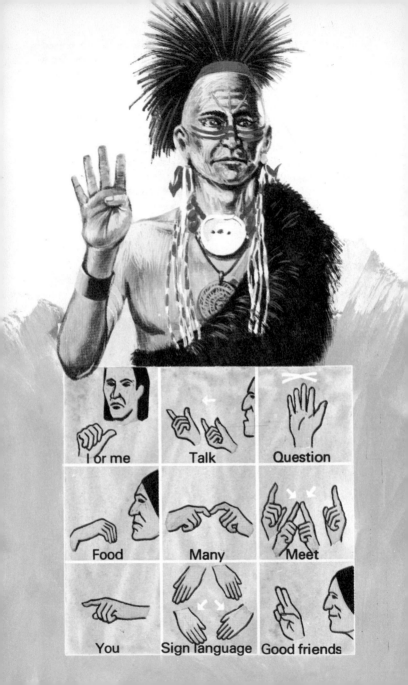

I or me

Talk

Question

Food

Many

Meet

You

Sign language

Good friends

speech and hearing *per se* that constitutes language competence. It is probable, however, that deaf mutes have at their disposal a language – sign language – which is just as rich as any spoken language. In the United States, American sign language (ASL) is used for communication between deaf human beings, and it is systematically taught to deaf children. It is entirely different from the deaf and dumb language used in Britain, that is, deaf mutes from these countries would be unable to communicate with one another.

ASL consists of hand-produced visual symbols called signs which are analogous to the words of a spoken language. Sign and speech differ in the organs that perceive them: the eye and ear respectively. The deaf cannot communicate unless they see one another. The deaf analyse language by sight whereas normal people analyse language by sound. As a result ASL is not simply a parallel or derivative of spoken English, it is an entirely different language. Just as in any spoken language a word is a particular combination of the phonemes of that language, so signs in ASL can be analysed into a combination of a few basic signs or cheremes. ASL consists of fifty-five cheremes and any sign is a combination of one or more of these. It was once thought that sign language lacked inflections and grammar; now, research has shown that in fact, like any spoken language, it possesses both of these. It seems then, that sign language has a rich structure and is based on rather different principles from spoken language.

These observations pose an interesting question with respect to the Whorfian hypothesis. If it is accepted that deaf mutes do in fact have a language at their disposal which is totally different from English, then the Whorfian hypothesis would predict that there would be some intellectual tasks which ASL users would perform better than normal English speakers. Studies with deaf children should therefore concentrate on finding intellectual tasks that would be better performed in one language rather than the other. Thus, if there were some intellectual tasks that are better performed by ASL users than normal children of the same age, this would afford some evidence for Whorf's hypothesis.

Indian sign language, used to overcome language and dialect differences between tribes.

Noam Chomsky, professor of linguistics at MIT.
B. F. Skinner, distinguished modern behaviourist.

Whorfian hypothesis and Bernstein

This observation also applies to Bernstein's work. In all the intellectual tasks that Bernstein has given to the children from the two social classes, the working-class child has on average fared the worst. If it is true, as Bernstein claims, that the two forms of language – the restricted and elaborated codes – serve different functions for the user, then they must also serve different intellectual functions in accordance with Whorf's hypothesis. If Bernstein is really correct, therefore, there must be some intellectual tasks for which restricted code users are superior to elaborated code users. If Bernstein, or anybody else, were to produce evidence that on some intellectual tasks working-class children were on average better than their middle-class peers, this would again be fairly strong evidence for the Whorfian hypothesis, and indirectly for Bernstein's theory.

There is one more point in connection with both the observed lag in deaf children compared with normal children, and the difference in average IQ between middle-class and working-class children. In both cases there does seem to be some connection between language and intellectual functioning. This does not mean, however, that language or the lack of it is the cause of the intellectual impairment. It could be, and very probably is, due to some factor in the working-class culture or the environment of the deaf child – lack of stimulation, malnutrition, lack of emotional security, alienation, or whatever – that causes *both* the observed intellectual and linguistic retardation. When Bernstein observes that there is a correlation between the type of code used and the average IQ, therefore, it might be better if more attention were devoted to finding out the impossible environmental factors that cause both the language impairment and intellectual retardation. Similarly, the fact that deaf children are lagging behind normal children might be nothing whatever to do with language, but have more to do with the loneliness and isolation with which these children are afflicted.

Chomsky and language

One of the most important single influences on the study of language is associated with the name of Noam Chomsky,

Consider the sentence:

SUE KICKED THE BALL

Phrase structure rules (or rewriting rules) determine the constituents of a sentence. The following phrase structure rules decompose the sentence into its surface structure:

1 Sentence → Noun phrase + Verb phrase
$$S \rightarrow Np + Vp$$

2 Noun phrase → Article + Noun
$$Np \rightarrow A + N$$

3 Verb phrase → Verb + Noun phrase
$$Vp \rightarrow V + Np$$

4 Noun → SUE, BALL
i.e N → SUE, BALL

5 Article → THE
i.e A → THE

6 Verb → KICKED
i.e V → KICKED

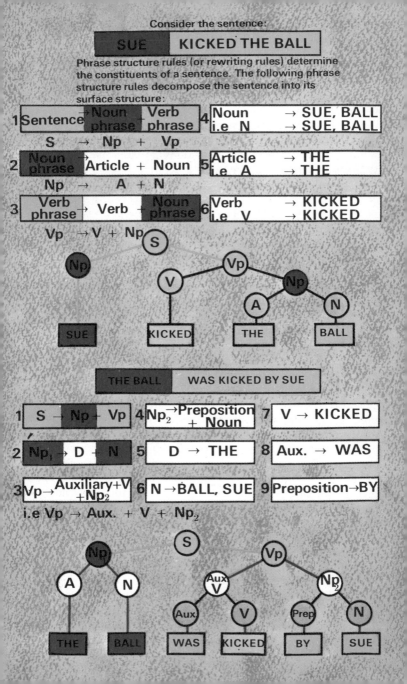

THE BALL WAS KICKED BY SUE

1 $S \rightarrow Np + Vp$

2 $Np_1 \rightarrow D + N$

3 $Vp \rightarrow \frac{Auxiliary + V}{+ Np_2}$
i.e $Vp \rightarrow Aux. + V + Np_2$

4 $Np_2 \rightarrow$ Preposition + Noun

5 $D \rightarrow THE$

6 $N \rightarrow BALL, SUE$

7 $V \rightarrow KICKED$

8 $Aux. \rightarrow WAS$

9 Preposition→BY

professor of linguistics at the Massachusetts Institute of Technology.

Skinner, in 1957, presented a behaviourist theory of how human beings acquire and learn language. Skinner suggested that language learning in children can be explained by exactly the same principles he had used to explain the way the rat or the pigeon learns to press a lever to contain food. The child, according to Skinner, starts with random babblings, and by shaping, imitation and instrumental conditioning, the correct words are learnt.

Chomsky demonstrated, however, that there were facts about language which learning theory was totally inadequate to cope with. He also argued strongly for an innate capacity to learn language in order to account for the amazing rapidity with which children do in fact acquire it.

The confrontation between these two views of language was not new, it was a revival of the question: Can we understand man as being simply the product of his environment? Skinner says you can and Chomsky says you cannot.

The seventeenth- and eighteenth-century philosophical debate on this question partly centred on the relationship between the human mind and its sense experience. Taking part in this debate were two opposing sides: the British empiricist philosophers and the Continental rationalist philosophers. The empiricists claim was that at birth the baby has a mind which starts as a blank slate, and all human knowledge is a result of learning and experience.

The rationalist philosophers, of whom Descartes was the most important exponent, argued that what a person knows and perceives is not simply a product of his environment. It was suggested instead that human minds are so constructed that they interpret the incoming stimuli in certain ways. The mind provides a mould on which is poured the incoming stimuli and experience. For the rationalists what is known and what is perceived is not simply a product of experience: it is connected with what is already present in the mind.

The learning theory of Skinner is a slightly modified version

Tree diagrams showing phrase structure of sentence: 'Sue kicked the ball' (*above*), and 'The ball was kicked by Sue' (*below*).

of eighteenth-century British empirical philosophy. These philosophers said, like the twentieth-century behaviourists say, that learning and human knowledge is simply the product of experience due to building up, by reinforcement and conditioning, of a set of associations and habits. Chomsky's theory of language is a reappearance, in the twentieth century, of the rationalist philosophers view of knowledge.

For Chomsky, an important problem for any theory of language is to explain the question: How do children obtain so complex a skill so quickly, so that any child has acquired a language, whatever it is, by the age of four?

Chomsky proposed that human languages are only superficially different, and that in some real way all natural languages derive from and are reflections of a universal grammar which imposes some restrictions on what constitutes a natural language. Thus English and Russian, though superficially quite different, are in fact permissible manifestations of a universal grammar. According to this view, the child has an 'innate language acquisition device' which enables it to tune in to the language of the culture.

Chomsky's transformational grammar

Chomsky's theory of transformational grammar is an attempt to solve the problem of creativity of language. The problem is: how is it that one can understand and generate an infinite number of sentences? As there cannot be a special rule for the

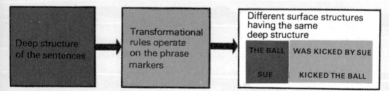

Sentences with different surface structures, but the same deep structure *(top)* and similar surface structure but different deep structure *(bottom)*

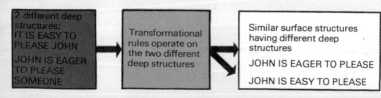

formation of every uttered sentence, then there must be a certain finite list of rules.

The grammar of a language, in Chomsky's view, is this finite set of rules which enables the individual to understand and generate an infinite number of possible sentences.

Deep structures and surface structures

An important part of Chomsky's theory is his distinction between the deep structure and the surface structure of a sentence. Roughly speaking, the surface structure of a sentence consists of the actual string of symbols or words. The deep structure is a more abstract way of representing grammatical relationships.

Two sentences can have different surface structures but the same deep structure: this happens when the two sentences have the same meaning. To illustrate this, consider the two sentences: Sue kicked the ball. The ball was kicked by Sue. Both these sentences have the same deep structure (one is essentially a paraphrase of the other), but both have different surface structures.

Transformational grammar has two kinds of rules: *phrase structure rules* and *transformational rules*.

A phrase structure rule determines the way in which a sentence can be sub-divided or rewritten. The constituents of this sub-division are typically phrases of the sentence, the verb phrase, the noun phrase, and so on. Phrase structure rules reveal the surface structure of the sentence.

Transformational rules are applied to the basic phrase markers. Phrase markers refer to those constituent phrases of the sentence already mentioned, the verb phrase, noun phrase, etc. The result of applying transformational rules to the phrase markers of a sentence results in a new surface structure which helps in understanding the sentence.

In the sentence, 'Sue hit the ball', a new surface structure may be generated by applying a transformational rule, called the passive transformation, which results in the surface structure, 'The ball was hit by Sue'.

All sentences in probably all languages are made up of both deep and surface structures. Transformational grammar shows the relationship between these two structures.

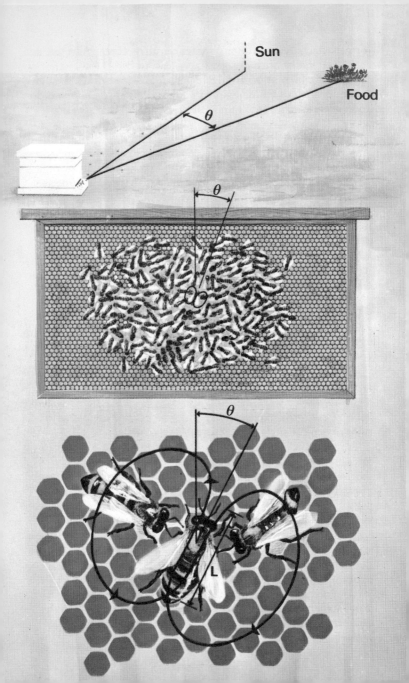

Evolution and language

There is no doubt that some animals do communicate with one another. Many animals have distress cries that signal the approach of danger. By a sequence of dance movements, honeybees can communicate to their hive-mates both the direction and distance of food sources from the hive. When food is close-by the dance pattern of the bees is in the shape of a circle. Food which is further away is indicated by a bee dancing in the form of a figure eight. The more rapid the dance, the further away the food.

Animal communication is not the same as language. A single item of information can be communicated either verbally or non-verbally. By using a system of arbitrary and conventional symbols as signs as in ASL, or sounds as in spoken language, language can convey an infinite variety of messages. It is this creative aspect of language, which is generated by a comparatively few grammatical rules, that Chomsky proposed was one of the hallmarks that separated human language ability from animal communication. In his book *Language and Mind*, Chomsky argues that language is a uniquely human attribute, and he has argued strongly against any analogy of animal communication systems with human language. For Chomsky, what is at issue is the uniqueness of man: of thought, mind and language.

Such a view presents a problem, however. Darwin's theory of evolution proposed that all living organisms have evolved from simpler ones by a process of natural selection. The doctrine of evolution is of prime importance to the psychologist: it not only has something to say about the way bodily structures have evolved, but also about the way that behaviour and intelligence have evolved from simpler structures.

When applied to man, evolutionary theory must explain unique features of human behaviour: his capacity to invent, to use tools, and to use language. Evolutionary theory declares that man is continuous with other animals and the problem is: if human language ability did not evolve from animal systems of communication, then where did it come

Using 'dance movements' a bee indicates to other hive members the location of food. L is proportional to the distance of the food.

from? It seems that it cannot be argued that language has evolved from the simpler forms of animal communication. Nowhere in any recorded language in any part of the world has there been evidence of language forms intermediate between animal communication and human language. All extinct languages, and the records of languages long since unused – classical Greek and Latin – show them to be fully developed languages in their own right.

Not long ago it was thought that there were three sorts of behaviour which were uniquely human: tool making, incest avoidance and language. Forms of the first two have now been found in the primate species, and now psychologists working in the United States claim that language too is no longer exclusive to human beings.

Washoe indicating 'hear' or 'listen' by ASL when trainer shows her a watch.

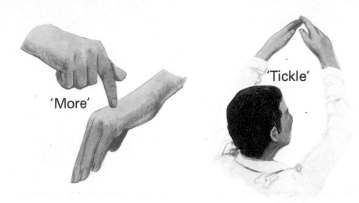

Two examples of sign words used to communicate with Washoe.

Teaching animals language

In an experiment conducted by a husband and wife team, Allen and Beatrice Gardner, a female chimpanzee called Washoe, then aged about twelve months, was taught ASL.

Previously attempts had been made to teach chimpanzees to vocalize but all these attempts had failed, and so the Gardners hit upon the idea of teaching Washoe sign language. For most of her waking hours she was in the presence of one or more human companions. The only form of communication was ASL, and all her trainers were required to master sign language, and were forbidden to converse in spoken language.

In the training session the signs were introduced to Washoe by shaping and instrumental conditioning. By the age of four years Washoe could use about eighty-five signs and form simple sentences like:

'Hurry, give me toothbrush'.

'Listen, dog'.

The last sentence was said when Washoe heard a dog bark outside the window.

The Gardner's work raised many questions. One is: To what extent is this a really genuine result? A troublesome problem in all psychology experiments is the effect that the experimenter himself has on the results. Most experimenters

have some idea about what result they expect and so they often unconsciously communicate their expectation of the result to the subjects taking part in the experiment. Psychologists have reported this effect not only for human subjects but for animal subjects as well.

A famous case of this was Clever Hans, the horse that astonished Germany and the rest of the world in the nineteenth century. Clever Hans was able, among other accomplishments, to do mental arithmetic. A questioner would ask the horse: 'Two plus two?' and Clever Hans would answer four by tapping his hoof four times.

It was eventually discovered that the horse could identify the unconscious cues (which signalled the correct answer) given by the questioner. Some questioners would imperceptibly nod their head the appropriate number of times and be quite unaware they were doing this, but this served as a signal to the horse to tap the appropriate number of times.

The question raised is: Are the feats of Washoe merely a more sophisticated Clever Hans effect? Are the trainers, unconsciously perhaps, giving out cues which signal the correct answer? The Gardners are not unaware of this problem and they seem satisfied, after taking precautions, that there is no Clever Hans error.

David Premack, a psychologist from the University of Santa Barbara, is teaching language to another female chimpanzee, Sarah. The elements of the language that Premack has used with Sarah are words expressed physically in the form of pieces of plastic that vary in shape, size and colour. These are metal-backed so that they will adhere to a magnetized wallboard or language board.

The 'words' are laid out on a table top and when forming sentences with the plastic shapes Sarah preferred to array them in a vertical column rather than a row, and she has kept to this Chinese convention. At the time of writing she has a vocabulary of some 130 words. In an early lesson, Sarah was taught to ask for fruit using her language board. At that time she knew the following words: 'give', take', 'apple', banana',

When hidden from the questioner, Clever Hans, the counting horse, failed to give the answer.

and 'Jim', 'Randy', 'Mary' (the names of her trainers).

If Sarah wanted an apple and Jim was present in the room, Sarah wrote up on the language board, 'Jim give apple Sarah'.

She also showed that she seemed able to understand sentence structure and not just word order. The trainer put the following message on the board:

'Sarah insert apple pail banana dish'.

To be able to make the correct interpretation, Sarah was required to put the apple in the pail and the banana in the dish, and not put the apple, the pail, and the banana in the dish. To do this correctly seems to imply that she understands sentence structure and not just word order.

The nature of language

These experiments force the question: What do we mean by language? What would a non-human organism, say a chimpanzee, or perhaps even a computer, have to accomplish in order to give evidence of possessing language ability?

At the very least its accomplishments would have to include the following. First, the ability to understand and generate sentences. Second, the ability of being able to recognize and use new words. Third, it must be able by means of language to learn more language. With these criteria alone Sarah passes with flying colours.

There are, however, more difficult questions of a philosophical character. Can Sarah think in the language she has been taught? To think successfully in a language means, at the very least, being able to generate the meaning of new words in the absence of their external representations. For Sarah to be able to match 'apple' with an actual apple may indicate she knows the meaning of the word, but it does not prove that when she is given the word 'apple' and no apple is present she can think apple, that is, mentally represent the meaning of the word to herself.

The linguistic concept of the imperative indicating an order or a command presents curious difficulties. If Sarah possesses this concept how is it different from the rat trained in the

Symbols used by Sarah and her trainers to communicate. A sentence, written vertically, is shown on the right. (After Premack and Premack)

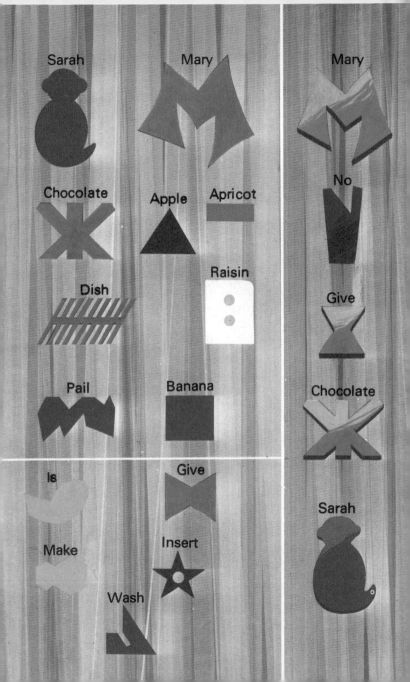

Skinner box to jump to the left every time it is presented with a red triangle, and to the right when it is presented with a rectangle? Can it be said that the rat also has the linguistic concept of the imperative?

Perhaps the most interesting problem of all is the extent to which our ideas of language will have to be revised if Sarah, or Washoe, teach other primates to communicate both with themselves and with other human beings.

Sarah carrying out the instruction in the symbolic message behind her.

THINKING

It is now well known that computers can be programmed to play chess, and while certainly they are well below the standard of expert players, they are better than most good ordinary players. It was the hope until recently that computer programs would attain grandmaster rating in the near future and that all that had to be done was to extend and develop existing programming techniques. This belief is now generally recognized to be mistaken, and although it is very probable that computer programs will attain grandmaster standard they will do so only by abandoning the traditional methods of programming.

In the traditional chess playing programs there was nothing in them which corresponded to 'knowledge' and 'understanding'. What was present was a mechanism for playing chess without knowing anything about the game or understanding it. These programs simply looked ahead a few moves and evaluated all the possible moves. The only knowledge present was the rules of chess and a set of stored chess openings.

Knowledge and artificial intelligence

Chess, like any other intellectual activity, has two components: the player's knowledge, and some techniques which apply this knowledge.

Until about 1970, all investigations into artificial intelligence (AI) were concerned with the application of knowledge, and so the research effort was devoted to finding methods whereby the direct implications of the players knowledge could be used. These methods consisted essentially of techniques for extracting the most from a minimal repertoire of stored facts.

Now the emphasis of workers in AI is to 'represent' a knowledge of a situation inside a machine, and the problem becomes one of how to represent what the computer knows about the world. This representation has two parts: there is, first, the problem of the representation of the world in such a form that the solutions of the problems can in principle be deduced from the facts expressed in the representation; and there is an *heuristic* part, such that on the basis of the information given a solution of the problem is decided faster than by a

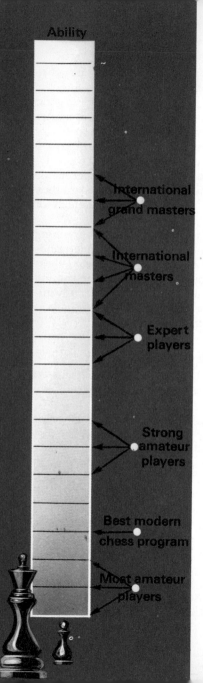

Ability

International grand masters

International masters

Expert players

Strong amateur players

Best modern chess program

Most amateur players

Ranking of chess players on the US Chess Federation scale, also showing the ability of chess programmed computers.

random searching method.

The traditional methods of programming intelligent machines were very vulnerable to a rapid growth problem – of the evaluation of a vast number of possible solutions (as in the chess programs). Programs which incorporate 'knowledge' offer methods of greatly reducing the process of search among these many possible methods of solution.

Programs which are now being developed in AI to represent knowledge rely essentially on description; that is, the describing of the essential features of a situation and the marking of abstract relationships between the objects and events of the world. To this end programming languages are now being developed for describing the significant features of situations. This representation problem in AI work is much the same as Piaget's notion of the internal representations that have to be built up in the mind of the growing child.

Popplestone's mini-world

In order to investigate the representation problem, workers in AI have constructed extremely simplified worlds, and one of the simplest so far built is that of Popplestone's of the University of Edinburgh.

Popplestone's world consists of only two places: 'here' and 'there'. There are a number of objects in this imaginary world. The world is inhabited by a robot consisting of only one hand which is capable of three actions: 'go to', which moves the hand to a stated place; 'pick up', which transfers into the hand any object chosen at random from the place where the hand is already situated; and 'let go'. Popplestone's task was to devise a 'knowledge' program for achieving a state of affairs in which at least one object was 'there'.

Artificial and real intelligence

Why build intelligent machines? What has this to do with human intelligence? The major difference between the physicists and biologists is that the physical scientist formulates theories of greater generality. A biologist is concerned only with organisms that actually exist; the physicist deals

Computers can be programmed to play a good game of chess, but as yet, cannot beat experts.

not only with actual organisms but the possible and therefore artificial.

AI approaches the study of organisms from the engineering point of view. That is, AI is concerned not only with organisms that actually exist, but also with the possible – in fact with the whole class of possible systems – whether they are living or not living. In this way intelligence can be looked at from an abstract point of view. It was only by an abstract study of the principles of flight – as formulated in mechanics and aerodynamics – that man was able to fly by means of an aeroplane, whereas his previous efforts at flying by donning feathers in the manner of birds failed. In the same way the hope is that an abstract study of intelligence in the manner in which workers in AI pursue it will give a greater understanding of human intelligence.

Language and the computer

After the end of the Second World War machine translation from one language into another became a major concern of the computer scientist. The idea that all the (albeit unsuccessful) translation programs embodied was a 'two-dictionary' approach, one for each language. The hope was that given enough alternative meanings for each word, together with the rules of grammar for each of the two languages and plenty of computer storage space, translation could be relatively easily accomplished. It was later discovered that this two-dictionary approach was inadequate, and machine translation research has now effectively ceased.

Instead, effort is now devoted to elucidating what is involved in understanding a 'natural' language like English, and Question-Answering systems are being developed with the aim of representing 'meaning' in a computer with reference to a circumscribed area of knowledge. In practice the 'knowledge base' problem is being tackled by constructing mini-worlds, so that the range of discourse between the system and human interrogator is effectively limited to objects in this mini-world.

Popplestone's mini-world robot has to move a specified object from 'here' to 'there'. Seemingly simple, it involved considerable programming problems.

Winograd's program for understanding natural language

Terry Winograd of the Massachusetts Institute of Technology has used a mini-world to help analyse what is involved in understanding language. The objects in this environment were geometric solids of different colours: rectangular wedges, pyramids and boxes. The sole inhabitant is a robot with an arm and an eye that can view this world. The robot can converse and be talked to by a human interrogator about its environment, and it can answer questions and move objects.

Here is one conversation between Winograd and the robot.

1 'Pick up a big red block.'
'O.K.'

2 'Grasp the pyramid.'
'I DON'T UNDERSTAND WHAT YOU MEAN.'
(There are three pyramids so the program does nothing.)

3 'Find a block which is taller than the one you are holding and put it into the box.'
(The system has now to work out what is meant by the pronouns 'one' and 'it' as well as to decide which particular box it is holding.)
'BY "IT", I ASSUME YOU MEAN THE BLOCK WHICH IS TALLER THAN THE ONE I AM HOLDING.'

4 'What does the box contain?'

'THE BLUE PYRAMID AND THE BLUE BOX.'

5 'What is the pyramid supported by?'

(It will be recalled that the system had answered 'the pyramid' by saying 'I don't understand which pyramid you mean', now it knows that Winograd must mean the one just mentioned.)

'THE BOX.'   (After Winograd 1970)

This kind of system suggests a very high degree of understanding and it would certainly pass Turing's test. Embedded in Winograd's language program are three kinds of knowledge: grammatical, inferential and semantic. Grammatical knowledge is the knowledge of the combination of words that are permissible in the language. Inferential knowledge refers to the knowledge of the world – and in Winograd's program to knowledge of the relationship between objects and actions in the mini-world of geometric objects. Semantic knowledge serves as a link between grammatical and inferential knowledge and as such leads to a grasp of the meaning of any particular sentence, and it can be seen from the conversation that the program takes into account the context in which any sentence is uttered.

The importance of Winograd's work is the recognition that grammar, semantics and inference are closely welded together, and the attempt it makes to understand how each of these kinds of knowledge relate to each other.

Winograd's mini-world of differently coloured geometrical objects.

WHAT SORT OF PSYCHOLOGY?

There always has been and probably always will be resistance to the idea that psychology should be regarded as a scientific enterprise with a need for rigour and experiment. A common alternative view is that because it is concerned with human beings and the ways in which they think, remember and experience, psychology should only be based on insights which are more intuitive and poetic.

Such a view has probably been compelled by the observation that artists, poets and novelists have been those traditionally concerned with exploring human nature, whereas scientists deal only with fact and their insights come not as a result of an imaginative leap, but as a consequence of the scientific laws being forced upon the minds by the sheer weight of impartial and objective data.

It is a fact, however, that the early behaviourists erred not because they insisted that psychologists should adopt scientific procedures, but because they did not propose bold imaginative theories to account for human behaviour. They were inhibited from doing so because of prevailing beliefs about the scientific enterprise: in particular, the doctrine that scientific laws leap into the mind of a neutral objective investigator – provided only that there is enough data. A related belief was that the task of the scientist is to prove theories.

The lack of objectivity in science

An alternative conception of science opposes the traditional view on almost all counts. Popper, the principal exponent of this newer view, insists that no matter how much data is collected no scientific law can ever be proved; there is always the possibility that at some future date an exception to the rule will be found. Hence science does not consist in proving theories; it consists rather of proposing imaginative hypotheses formulated in such a way that, although they cannot be proved, they can in principle be disproved by emperical tests.

On this view scientific theories are tested by systematic attempts to refute them. The task, therefore, is to propose imaginative theories and to make forecasts of what future observations or experiments will show. If these experiments go against the predictions, then the theory has been disproved.

Another important consequence of Popper's criticism is the denial of the possibility of objective observations. To say that a psychologist goes into the laboratory and simply observes with no preconceptions is false. Rather, the view is that all scientific discoveries originate from an imaginative guess as to what the truth might be. His observations are guided by hypotheses which direct the attention to what to observe and what to leave out.

It is only in the process of testing hypotheses that objectivity and the empirical method are essential, and it is here that the imagination of the scientist has to submit to external reality and to disappointing fact: and it is here also that the still point between the wish of the creative imagination and the reality must be located and maintained.

What do psychologists do?

A basic prerequisite for a psychologist today is a university degree in psychology. After a first degree it is usual to pursue some form of specialist postgraduate training for most careers.

It is useful to think of psychologists as being employed in one of four main areas: industry, the social services (including education and hospitals), the Civil Service and academic psychology.

The degree course in psychology in Britain is much the same in all the universities. It usually involves three or four years of study for an honours degree and includes physiology, statistics, experimental design, experimental psychology and social psychology. Social psychology, to which not much mention has been made in this book, includes the study of attitudes, the individual in society and personality formation.

In industry, psychologists are employed in advertising, market research and personnel selection. In all these applications the psychologist is brought in to predict and explain buyer behaviour. In advertising and market research he is called upon to advise about attitudes to products and why consumers have preferences for one product rather than another. In personnel work the psychologist is primarily interested in job specification – the analysis of the task – and this will involve him in developing aptitude tests to find the kind of personality best suited for a particular job.

University

Industrial psychology

Prison psychology

Clinical psychology

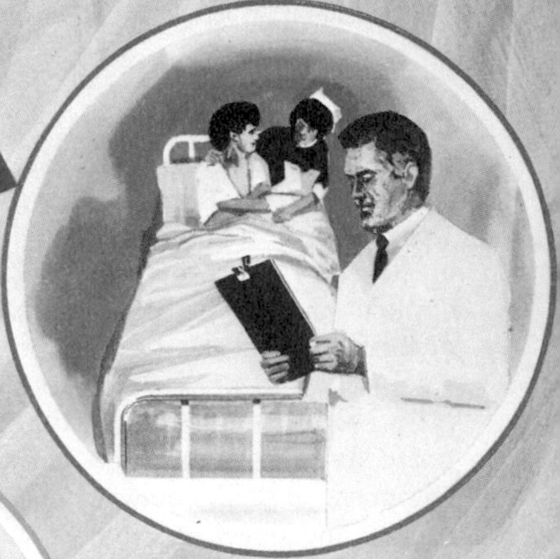

Academic psychology

Some of the roles of psychologists in contemporary society.

The social services employ by far the greatest number of psychologists – in the hospital services, child guidance centres, and local educational authorities. Most of the career openings in the social services require some form of post-graduate training. Educational psychologists are usually trained and experienced teachers, with a degree in psychology plus a postgraduate qualification in educational psychology. Most of their work is concerned with children who for one reason or another have behavioural and emotional difficulties either at school or at home. Clinical psychologists are usually attached to hospitals for the mentally ill and their job is mainly concerned with diagnosis, assessment (the administering of tests to determine IQ and personality) and treatment, which usually involves some form of psychotherapy. Typically, the clinical psychologist works with a team headed by a psychiatrist. The main difference between him and the clinical psychologists is that psychiatrists have a medical training with some postgraduate training in abnormal psychology.

The Civil Service employs psychologists of all kinds, and they are to be found working in prisons, the armed forces, personnel selection, the various government sponsored research organizations (such as the Road Research Laboratory) and the Medical Research Council Units. Civil Service psychologists carry out work which ranges from work of a very applied nature, for example the designing of surveys to determine people's attitudes about specific aspects of government policy, to work which involves 'pure research'.

By now it should be clear that the word 'psychologist' does not convey very much. It is rather like calling someone an engineer – it can cover almost everything from designing rockets and aeroplanes to the civil engineer who builds bridges and tunnels. In psychology the same is true; there are those who work with children and animals, and there are those where research interest involves them in work with physiology and computers and linguistics.

Nowhere is this multiplicity of interests more evident than among academic psychologists and especially those working in the universities. An academic psychologist working in a university both teaches and does research – indeed, most of the research reported in this book was carried out in various universities around the world.

GLOSSARY

Associative learning: behaviour pattern developed by linking stimulus with response.

Cerebral cortex: superficial grey matter of the brain.

Chereme: basic unit of American Sign Language.

Conditioning: process whereby a definite response is elicited by a definite stimulus.

Computer program: sequence of commands causing a computer to perform desired calculation.

Culture free test: intelligence designed to eliminate bias due to culture differences.

Elaborated code: the way higher socio-economic groups in Britain communicate with each other, according to Bernstein.

Heredity: transmission of genetic characteristics from parents to offspring.

Heuristic method: method of problem solving, which eliminates searching all possible solutions.

Hippocampus: region of brain situated under the cerebellum.

Hypothesis: provisional theory to explain observed facts.

Hysteria: psychoneurotic disorder arising from conflict and repression.

Innate: present in the individual at birth; unlearned.

Learning: a change of behaviour resulting from practice or experience.

Linguistic: relating to language.

Memory: assimilation of experiences which modify future behaviour.

Morpheme: smallest meaningful element in a language.

Neurosis: disorder whereby anxiety and obsessions dominate the personality.

Objective test: test independent of subjective evaluation by the tester.

Optic chiasma: region where right optic nerve crosses to left side of brain and vice versa.

Pattern recognition: process whereby viewed objects are perceived by the brain.

Perception: process of becoming aware of objects via the sense organs.

Phobia: dread or fear, usually morbid, of some object or situation.

Phoneme: smallest individual speech sound in a language.

Phrase structure: sub-divisions of a sentence; noun phrase, verb phrase, etc.

Polarized light: light waves travelling in one plane only.

Prism: transparent body which deflects light rays passing through it.

Psychoanalysis: psychotherapeutic method of treating certain neuroses.

Psychosis: severe mental disease with various origins.

Restricted code: the way lower socio-economic groups

in Britain communicate with each other, according to Bernstein.

Retina: light-sensitive layer of the eye.

Schizophrenia: psychotic disorder characterized by dissociation and delusions.

Size constancy: tendency for familiar objects to appear natural size despite distance.

Split-brain: brain in which the hemispheres are separated surgically.

Subjective test: test whose results are open to interpretation by the tester.

Template: already existing record or pattern in the brain, to which perceived objects are compared in the recognition process.

BOOKS TO READ

The Intelligent Eye by R. L. Gregory. Weidenfeld and Nicolson, London, 1970. A very good introduction to the psychology of perception and beautifully illustrated.

Behaviour by D. E. Broadbent. University Paperbacks, Methuen, London, 1964. This is probably the best introductory text on psychology to date; written by one of Britain's most distinguished experimental psychologists.

Sense and Nonsense in Psychology by H. J. Eysenck. Penguin Books, London, 1957. Professor Eysenck has written a series of books for Penguin, all of which are worth reading.

The Politics of Experience and The Bird of Paradise by R. D. Laing. Penguin Books, London, 1967. This book is a good introduction to some of the works of Laing.

The Psychopathology of Everyday Life by S. Freud. Benn, London, 1966. This gives a lucid and fascinating account of some case histories.

The Interpretation of Dreams by S. Freud. Allen and Unwin, London, 1967. This is one of Freud's major works.

An Introduction to the Psychology of Language by Peter Herriot. Methuen, London, 1970. This book gives an introduction to Chomsky and transformational grammar.

Language and Mind by Noam Chomsky. Harcourt and Brace, New York, 1969. This is a readable account of Chomsky's own work, and its significance to studies of the mind.

The Nature of Mind by A. J. P. Kenny, H. C. Longuet-Higgins, J. R. Lucas and C. H. Waddington. Edinburgh University Press, 1972. This is an extremely lively book based on a set of discussions by two philosophers – one a worker in artificial intelligence, the other a biologist.

INDEX

Page numbers in **bold**
type refer to illustrations.

SOME OTHER TITLES IN THIS SERIES

Arts
Antique Furniture/Architecture/Art Nouveau for Collectors/Clocks
and Watches/Glass for Collectors/Jewellery/Musical Instruments/
Porcelain/Pottery/Silver for Collectors/Victoriana

Domestic Animals and Pets
Budgerigars/Cats/Dog Care/Dogs/Horses and Ponies/Pet Birds/Pets
for Children/Tropical Freshwater Aquaria/Tropical Marine Aquaria

Domestic Science
Flower Arranging

Gardening
Chrysanthemums/Garden Flowers/Garden Shrubs/House Plants/
Plants for Small Gardens/Roses

General Information
Aircraft/Arms and Armour/Coins and Medals/Espionage/Flags/
Fortune Telling/Freshwater Fishing/Guns/Military Uniforms/Motor
Boats and Boating/National Costumes of the world/Orders and
Decorations/Rockets and Missiles/Sailing/Sailing Ships and Sailing
Craft/Sea Fishing/Trains/Veteran and Vintage Cars/Warships

History and Mythology
Age of Shakespeare/Archaeology/Discovery of: Africa/The American
West/Australia/Japan/North America/South America/Great Land
Battles/Great Naval Battles/Myths and Legends of: Africa/Ancient
Egypt/Ancient Greece/Ancient Rome/India/The South Seas/
Witchcraft and Black Magic

Natural History
The Animal Kingdom/Animals of Australia and New Zealand/
Animals of Southern Asia/Bird Behaviour/Birds of Prey/Butterflies/
Evolution of Life/Fishes of the world/Fossil Man/A Guide to the
Seashore/Life in the Sea/Mammals of the world/Monkeys and
Apes/Natural History Collecting/The Plant Kingdom/Prehistoric
Animals/Seabirds/Seashells/Snakes of the world/Trees of the
world/Tropical Birds/Wild Cats

Popular Science
Astronomy/Atomic Energy/Chemistry/Computers at Work/The
Earth/Electricity/Electronics/Exploring the Planets/Heredity/
The Human Body/Mathematics/Microscopes and Microscopic Life/
Physics/Psychology/Undersea Exploration/The Weather Guide